781.66   Hopkins, Del.
HOP
         Careers as a rock
         musician.

$14.95   940742

CAREERS AS A
ROCK MUSICIAN

By
DEL HOPKINS
MARGARET HOPKINS

The Rosen Publishing Group, Inc.
NEW YORK

Published in 1993 by The Rosen Publishing Group, Inc.
29 East 21st Street, New York, NY 10010

First Edition

Hopkins, Del.
    Careers as a rock musician / by Del Hopkins, Margaret
Hopkins. — 1st ed.
        p.   cm.
    Includes bibliographical references and index.
    Summary: Evaluates careers in rock music and discusses the
preparation, competition, and lifestyles of rock musicians.
    ISBN 0-8239-1518-2   ISBN 0-8239-1725-8 (paperback)
    1. Rock music—Vocational guidance. [1. Rock music—
Vocational guidance. 2. Vocational guidance.] I. Hopkins,
Margaret, 1929-. II. Title.
    ML3795.H77
    781.66'023'73—dc20   92-42615
                                                      CIP
                                                   AC MN

Manufactured in the United States of America

About the Authors

Del Hopkins supplied the information for this book from his work in the rock music business over the past eighteen years.

He began to study the drums when he was in second grade. By the 8th grade he was in his first rock band. He had just graduated from high school when he and a band played their first six-week booking. Three years later he went on tour with a trio that entertained in resort hotels throughout the West.

Del and his wife, Kris, took their honeymoon in California and decided to stay. In the following years he played drums with several Los Angeles underground bands, including 45 Grave, VoxPop, Passionel, and The Jeff Dahl Band. With these bands he made fifteen records, which are sold in Europe, England, and Australia. "Just Like Your Mom" by VoxPop was a hit in both Los Angeles and Italy. He also recorded the musical score for a movie.

Del is in the middle of a career change. He found that the planning needed to do tours in the rock music business was transferable. He and Kris currently operate their own tour company escorting European travelers throughout the West. In his spare time he does color drawings of surrealistic landscapes.

Margaret Hopkins organized Del's information to write this book. He spoke his memories into a tape recorder, and she arranged his thoughts for readers.

Margaret Hopkins was graduated from the University of Oregon with a B.S. and an M.S. in Education. She taught Art to 7th and 8th graders for three years, in high school for seven years, and in college for two years. Several of her articles on teaching have been published in professional journals.

She and her husband, Joe, have three children. While she brought them up, she served as chairman of the City Beautification Commission and spearheaded the opening of a church preschool. When the children left home, Margaret entered a new career.

Art and teaching remain her chief interest, as she is now a docent, guiding visitors through the art museum. She also teaches docent trainees.

Writing this book has been very rewarding to Margaret Hopkins as she learned about her son Del's unique choice of occupation. It was also an excuse to visit often and hug her grandchild.

Contents

Introduction   vi
1. Preparation for a Career in Rock Music   1
2. Steps to Live Performance   25
3. Competition for a Recording Contract   43
4. Life-styles of Musicians   81
5. The Job Market in Rock   95
6. Evaluating a Career in Rock   118
   Glossary   130
   Appendixes
       A. *Bookkeeping*   135
       B. *Recording Contract*   138
   For Further Reading   150
   Index   152

Introduction

Perhaps you are now where I once was as a high school student. Graduation was approaching, and also my last free meal at home. There were hints that I ought to be making up my mind about what kind of work I wanted to do. It was expected of me to pitch in like everyone else to make a living. College was the only choice besides a job, but that, too, required a career focus. There was no way to avoid it—I had to start thinking about work.

I had been working all along, but it was so much fun and so fulfilling that I never considered it drudgery, which is what I thought work meant in those days. By the time I became a senior, I had played in several rock bands, spent most of my evenings practicing with a group, and had performed in gigs for money.

My classmates seemed to like me for my music, which was fine because I wasn't exactly on the principal's list for good grades, nor was I a star quarterback. Up to then my life in music had been more like a high school social activity; but now, with all the pressure for a career, I began to think otherwise. I looked everywhere for information on how to get ahead in the rock business.

The school library was no help at all. There were books on music careers leading to opera or symphony, but none leading to popular music forms such as rock, country, or jazz. The differences are too great to make comparisons between the two career paths. If I had been interested in academic music, I would have stayed in the school band and planned on attending college. So, with no guidance available from the adult world, I relied on the advice of friends and questionable experts. My journey of trial and error through the real world of rock has given me one certainty—it's not like high school. If you are considering a career in the rock business, please read on.

The purpose of this book is to provide an inside view of the music business behind the glitter of rock concerts and compact discs. I shall also tell some true-life experiences about work as a rock musician so that you will not have to rely on speculation. Such a book would have been of immeasurable help during my eighteen years to date as a professional musician.

1

Preparation for a Career in Rock Music

DEVELOPMENT OF INSTRUMENTAL SKILLS

The path to becoming a rock musician is different from, but no less demanding than, that to becoming a traditional musician.

A seven-year-old became interested in playing the drums. He was watching a parade of about twenty boys and girls, not much older than he, each playing a snare drum. Something stirred in him when he heard the beat approaching, and from that moment on he loved drums. He begged his mother for lessons, to which she agreed, but she wasn't about to buy an instrument. First, she wanted to know if this was going to be a passing fad. He went through several months of lessons beating on a rubber pad, not too happily because he wanted the real thing. Even so, those lessons laid a necessary foundation for his music career. He learned the basics of handling drumsticks, wrist movements, and the importance of timing.

The following year in school he joined the percussion section of the school band. A drum was rented for him, and he took more lessons. As he participated in concerts and parades, his parents saw that this was not a passing fancy, so they bought him an instrument. They were already replacing broken drumsticks on a regular basis.

1

But they didn't realize that his sights were set on something more than the school band, so they didn't go along when he asked for a full drumset.

When he entered junior high he got a newspaper route and one by one purchased a bass drum, tomtoms, and cylinders. By the summer before entering high school, he was practicing with two neighbors who played guitars. Their rehearsal room was his bedroom, with the windows closed to prevent bothering the neighbors. The parents insisted that the boys wear cotton earplugs to save their hearing. One of the trio was a salesman type who found a gig to play, as their parents looked on.

Not quite matching the Beatles in that first performance didn't discourage them. But entering a new high school with so many other challenges distracted them from the band for a while. He studied alone to learn his instrument thoroughly. He listened to records of good drummers, analyzed them, and tried to play just like them.

By his sophomore year, the old band was practicing again. They had a definite objective: to play in the band jamboree sponsored by the city park. That is how they were discovered by all the other musicians in school. They were asked individually to practice with other bands and so went their separate ways. He regrets that the original band has never gotten together again, but he does not regret the opportunity to play with many other musicians.

Making rock music with another person is a basic act of cooperation. It is one thing to play alone and another thing to integrate with another musician's part to create a new sound. Multiply that by the number of people in the band, and making rock music becomes a very complex operation. Jamming may sound to others like aimless fooling around, but it serves a useful purpose.

2

Each musician is developing sensitivity to others' musical ways and styles. He does this while contributing his own part to the whole.

Not every band this young musician practiced with led to gigs and money. They did enable him to grow in group cooperation within the basic elements of all music. Rock music focuses on group sound and the democratic development of that sound. By comparison, academic music focuses on individual parts and following the leader to achieve a unified sound. A career in rock music does not require a college degree, but skill in group cooperation is a necessity.

The story of the young musician is offered to illustrate the years needed to develop skills in rock music. It is important to take the time for lessons and practice, and to play in different bands and with many other musicians, for the average life span of an unprepared musician is less than five years.

There are, of course, exceptions to every rule. A friend used to hang around the high school rock band when they practiced. He didn't play an instrument, but he was in their faces continually, asking for something he could do to be a part of the group. He would fool around trying to sing and doing weird things with various instruments. He would dress up in totally uninhibited clothes to do an act that might enhance the music. Today he is in Hollywood doing the same thing on a larger scale. He managed to pick up some skills on the guitar and drums and along with his musical clowning ability is doing very well. For him, the driving force is acting like a court jester, and everything else is incidental to that purpose. For the person whose motivation is a career in rock music, lessons on an instrument, individual practice, and group practice are still the rule.

SEARCH FOR A PROFESSIONAL BAND

The search for just the right combination of musicians to form a career rock band is a discipline that can take days or years to accomplish. As one band member said, "Musicians don't think of bands as business. They are not thinking whether it will sell or if it is a product. They are thinking 'Let's make music,' and that is a big problem." Career implies the need to gain financial independence, to be able to support a family, and to prepare for retirement. Those are the goals of a career musician; therefore, objectives have to be redirected to turn a hobby into a business. Most bands formed in high school are based on friendship, but career bands are more specific about talent, skills, and the profit motive. Newspaper ads, bulletin board items, networking, and referral services are some of the avenues to follow in the search for people of like mind.

The classified section of the newspaper may have a column for musicians advertising for other musicians. Some larger cities have entertainment weekly newspapers that carry classified ads. Trade papers that run music business information are *Billboard, Cashbox,* and *Variety.* Ads can be found in as many places as an ad to sell a car, so the band searcher has to be alert for opportunities.

Music shops that cater to rock musicians often maintain a bulletin board on which a band can advertise for an instrumentalist or an instrumentalist can advertise himself as available for work. Other bulletin boards can be found in Laundromats and in restaurants where musicians congregate. The drawback is that one's private business becomes public and may generate nuisance calls. Posting a phone number is preferable to posting an address.

Networking is the most dignified way to find a band, and it probably brings more lasting results. In the

4

course of learning this trade, a musician makes many friends who know his or her style and can make a personal recommendation. Practicing with many musicians over the years is an investment that pays back eventually with a network of friends. Each has a circle of musician friends who know of openings in other bands. Jamming with others helps in gaining skills and making contacts. The trick in networking, however, is not letting contacts lapse. Job-hunting means calling old musician friends to see how they are doing, making dates to get together, and checking for openings. Then repeat the process in a month.

In a metropolitan area like Los Angeles, it is possible to find entrepreneurs who run musician referral services for a fee. Such services exist because one-time engagements are more common than long-term. Musicians who work through such a service, similar to Kelly Girl for temporary office work, must have a wide repertoire and be extremely flexible. Just as a Kelly Girl may move from temporary help to a permanent position, it is possible for a good musician mix on a temporary assignment to turn into a permanent arrangement.

A musician cannot sit in front of television every day and expect a band to find him. Those in high income brackets may come closest to that utopian dream by hiring a manager and paying him a cut of every check received. The beginning professional musician must be like a detective in a relentless search for a band with the right combination of personalities, instrumental skills, and organization.

Auditioning With a Band

The key to placement in a band is a good audition. Steps leading to the audition are the ad/referral response and practice with the band's tape. After the audition, the musician's own emotional response to the band's

5

decision, whether acceptance or rejection, needs attention and understanding.

When an interesting band opening becomes available, musicians respond to it in the manner specified in the ad. If a phone number is given, they are prepared to give a list of credits during the phone call. If an address is given, a résumé of experience and copies of newspaper clippings covering performances are sent to that address. The originals are not sent because they probably would not be returned. Only the most important clippings are included with the résumé.

If the band is interested, they give the musician a tape of their music and set a time for the audition. The musician practices on his instrument to the sound of the tape as much as needed to do the job well. For one audition, a bass player was given tape recordings of forty songs. She said of the experience, "On previous auditions I had worked out a system for making notes on a song so I could perform its various parts in the correct sequence. Since this band was already successful, I truly wanted to fill the opening, so I made my notes and practiced all forty songs. The band was amazed that I could keep up with them for so long, but it was all due to the note system to aid my memory. I was invited to join them, and that incident greatly improved my reputation as a musician."

The makeup of current popular bands is as varied as are instruments. An average band has a guitar, a bass, drums, and keyboard. There also might be harmonicas, a kazoo, and a guy who chases a poodle with a big stick. The musician's appraisal of the band begins with the audition tape, determining whether the instrument combination is one he or she can live with.

Musicians take their own instrument to auditions; because it is familiar, they can make their best appearance with it. An exception might be that a band will have drums set up, since drums are somewhat difficult to move. The band evaluates the musician for command of instrument and how he or she fits in with their music. They check whether this person would personally fit in with them. Personality may not seem a fair way to access a musician, yet this kind of conflict has ruined bands before. They will be looking for a compatible person with like skills and similar goals, because people have to be in a good frame of mind to make music together.

Handling Rejection

Putting oneself on display to be judged by others is never easy. Gifted writers, artists, actors, dancers, and musicians have passed unknown into history because they couldn't stand up to rejection. To be chosen is great, but not to be chosen, especially when a musician wants to be in a certain band, is a minor death. Musicians must learn to respond to rejection in a profitable way, because it is part of the business.

Some musicians try to hide the fact that they were turned down and won't admit they ever auditioned. They bury the memory and pain and try to forget it ever happened. A healthier response is to feel the pain and learn from it. By asking for honest reasons why the band chose someone else, they may gain insight into changes that would bring success. Rejection is not something to be ashamed of, but an opportunity for growth.

Some people become angry and consider ways to get revenge. One angry musician started uncomplimentary rumors about the rejecting band. Another stole their instruments, and a third took out his anger on his parents. A more positive way to deal with anger is to beat a punching bag until the feeling goes away. Or write an angry letter but don't send it. When the urge

7

to do harm subsides, ask for honest reasons so that changes can be made.

Others become depressed at being turned down. They ask themselves why they bothered in the first place. They feel that all efforts to get ahead are useless, as they always lose. Hopelessness saps the energy to try again. Such people need a friend with an encouraging attitude to boost sagging spirits during low times. When acceptance finally returns, they can think positively about the reasons for rejection and changes that need to be made.

No one likes to be rejected, yet it is part of the rock musician's life. Since rejection cannot be avoided, musicians try to avoid useless, dead-end habits. Instead, they interpret the lost opportunity as preparation for a better opportunity up ahead. They learn from it and move forward.

EVALUATION OF THE BAND

The musician also makes decisions about the personality aspect of the band. No rules can be offered, because preference in company is highly individual. Only the applicant knows if the members are people he or she can work with in close association. When a keyboardist first went to New York, he auditioned with a band that had a former play director as songwriter. This songwriter did not play an instrument but popped around like a grasshopper poking and pulling at everyone to make the music louder and faster. It was a kind of behavior that wore out the keyboardist's nerves. He decided to wait for a better opportunity.

Just as job-seekers evaluate whether a company will enhance their career, so musicians evaluate bands. The trouble is that musicians are artists who seldom understand business; consequently, they don't know what to look for. They don't know how to judge a group according to their own long-term needs. If musicians don't see themselves as professional, or give away their talent because they like to hang out with the gang, the following points of evaluation will not interest them. But to earn income by rock music they have to make judgments about band management, money, and bookkeeping.

These questions need not sound like a drill sergeant forcing answers out of a buck private. Concerns can be discussed in a casual way as part of general conversation with members of the group. When the audition is over and the new musician has been selected, it is time to ask questions that have not been answered. Before an agreement is reached, the band's practices about leadership, income and bookkeeping, and outside help need to be explained to the musician's satisfaction. If musicians fail to ask questions about these issues, they are assumed to be ignorant about business and therefore vulnerable to shady practices.

Leadership

A spirit of equality prevails in rock bands that is unlike other music groups. Members see themselves as needed and valued, on a par with everyone else, though each performs differently. They all work together to create music without hierarchy, so it is sometimes difficult to determine who is doing the work of leader.

There are leaders of ideas, such as the songwriter, though all members eventually help to create and finish the song. There are leaders of people, such as the manager, though all members help to find places to practice. And there are leaders in persuasion, such as the salesman, though all play a part in promoting the band's popularity.

The problem in rock groups is not the songwriter and the creation of music, but the business. Band members may not have talent in management, sales, and bookkeeping. Perhaps they can't afford to hire help. Then the most responsible person in the group struggles to supply what is lacking. That person may not be very good at it. He or she may not be a designated leader but does the work of a leader because it has to be done along with making music.

Some people are prone to look after the needs of the whole group. They volunteer to find places to rehearse, make travel arrangements, collect and distribute money to the band. They don't have to be asked because thinking about group needs rather than individual needs is easy for them. If they cannot get around to doing everything, they ask for help or organize a cooperative effort by the group. When managerial talent is missing, the band is disorganized about everything it does.

Having a manager in a beginning band does not mean that everyone else is free of responsibility. A drummer tells of an unhappy experience with a manager. "She wanted to upgrade the band's equipment, so she arranged to trade in my drumset for a new one. The next thing I knew I was kicked out of the band, and she sold my new drumset. I took the whole band to justice court over it. It turned out that when she signed the trade-in papers she officially owned the equipment. But the judge awarded me the money to buy a secondhand set because it was so unfair." A manager is no substitute for each musician's learning about business.

Even though all may operate in a democratic spirit in rehearsals, the audience wants to see and hear a band leader in live performance. This person is the Master of Ceremonies, so he or she should be articulate and able to speak persuasively enough to hold attention between sets. If the music is dark and foreboding, then the leader should reflect that—or whatever the total band's style happens to be. This person is essentially a salesperson who can convince others. The salesperson arranges for advertising, prepares a press kit, networks with other music professionals, and finds places to perform. If no one in the group has sales ability, the band never seems to move beyond rehearsing.

"The very first band I was in had a great agent. He had to be, because we were a lousy band." A professional bass player told his story about music salesmen or agents. "We were only thirteen or fourteen years old. The lead guitarist had connections in his church, so he arranged for us to play at their dances and once at a picnic in the park. We knew only a few songs, so we'd play them over and over. I remember one was 'House of the Rising Sun'—we played it about every twenty minutes. People kept coming up and asking if we knew anything else.

"We were more interested in how many cords we had dangling around the stage. One of the guys used to bring extra cords to make it look like we were swimming in electronics. We made giant amplifier boxes for our tiny little speakers so we would look more like the bands on television.

"He was right out there finding places to play—mostly school and church dances. He was the kind of guy who dreamed of having his own company someday. He always got paying jobs, too—not much, but something."

Finding someone in the group with the ability to keep financial records should not be difficult. Tests show that people with musical ability are often talented in math, too. Money is advanced to pay expenses, and money earned is divided among the band members according to previous agreement. If the band is organized on a partnership model, the bookkeeper records all money exchanges in a journal. He or she balances the bank account and makes financial reports to the partners. In some band businesses, the bookkeeper files tax reports with the government.

It is better to resolve these issues up front than to waste time and effort with a dead-end band; the transition of the musician's career from play to professional is at stake.

INCOME AND BOOKKEEPING

Before a musician joins a band he or she should have a clear picture of how money earned by the band will be handled. All entertainers need to be vigilant about finances. The comedian Redd Foxx and the country-western singer Dottie West are two instances of show people who were not careful. Both were superstars who didn't look beyond the paycheck that was handed to them. They knew that expenses were being deducted from their earnings, but they didn't know what those expenses were. The Internal Revenue Service eventually seized their houses and other possessions to pay taxes. It was a crushing experience for entertainers who had worked hard all their lives, only to face a mountain of debt in their old age. They urged all young people to study, to understand the business side of entertainment.

The following guidelines should help the beginning professional musician to think more clearly about business organization and accounting. Books and classes are available if a musician is interested in more detail. Appendix A provides an example of simplified bookkeeping that a start-up band might use to keep money records straight.

Business means the buying and selling of a commodity for the purpose of making a profit. The band's commodity is music; they are selling their music when they play for money. Novice musicians are accustomed to producing art. It is necessary to shift mental gears and start thinking of this art as a product for sale.

A band can make either a profit or a loss on the sale of their music. Suppose they have paid out $200 in expenses before they are booked to perform. If they earn $150, they have a loss of $50. They will have to perform twice in order to cover expenses and earn money. If instead they earned $300 on their first performance, they would have made a profit of $100.

The aim of the band is to sell their music for a higher price, but they also must keep control of expenses. Earnings before expenses have been deducted is called Gross Income: earnings after expenses have been deducted is called Net Income. Rehearsal hall rent is a necessary expense, unless a band member has a basement or other sound-controlled place to practice. Fliers, posters, and newspaper ads are advertising expense. If the band plays out of town, travel and hotel expenses must be deducted. Miscellaneous supplies such as bookkeeping ledger sheets, business cards, or recording tapes are expenses. The band may agree to telephone answering service as an expense. It is all right to object to expenses, because that is what eats up profit. If the manager, who usually pays the bills, proves to be extravagant, complain.

More often band members have no idea what expenses are being deducted from earnings. They neither receive nor ask for an income statement. Because no one seemed to care, one manager made long-distance telephone calls from hotels and wrote them down as tour expenses. Another ran personal classified ads and charged them as advertising expenses to the band. The risk of dishonesty is reduced if the person who handles the money is accountable to others in the band. That is why the musician acting as manager signs the checks and the musician acting as bookkeeper records all financial exchanges. Information regarding the expenses deducted from earnings is given to the musicians in income statements (see Appendix A). These are handed out with every paycheck.

Rock bands are generally paid immediately after a one-night engagement. They are seldom paid by the week unless the band has a contract for a longer period of time. Payments are often made in cash, as club operators would rather not carry money to the bank at night. No income taxes or social security taxes are withheld, so the band or the musician is reponsible for paying those taxes to both state and federal governments. If it is expected that each band member will earn more than $600 for the year, the band withholds taxes. If not, the individual member estimates and pays his own taxes. The Internal Revenue Service and Social Security Administration have toll-free telephone numbers and are very helpful with answers to questions. If the band bookkeeper fails to recognize tax responsibilities, the musicians will suffer the consequences years later when they try to collect social security payments in old age.

Most bands are organized as one of two kinds of business organization, proprietorship or partnership. The former is set up like a company, with an owner who hires musicians as if they were employees. They are engaged in the creation of music, but they have no say in the business operations other than to collect an hourly wage for time put in. That wage is also paid for rehearsal and travel time. If the band makes a profit, the musician collects no more than the previously agreed hourly wage.

Musicians employed by the motion picture industry are usually members of the union. They are paid approximately $170 for the first three hours of a recording session. Record companies pay their studio musicians approximately $200 for the first three hours of a recording session.

Rock bands have tended to stay nonunion and form business partnerships instead. The musicians invest a certain amount of money to pay for start-up costs. Each member takes responsibility for an extra business-related job in addition to music. Then all share equally in the profits. At regular intervals they discuss, evaluate, and make suggestions for the improvement of their business. Each can make from $30 to $300 for each engagement and more, depending on the band's star power.

Rip-off artists abound in the major recording cities. The competition to join a band makes aspiring young musicians afraid to ask questions that might put their acceptance in jeopardy. They settle for business arrangements that cost them hours in travel time and practice. Their instruments depreciate with use, and repairs or improvements are at their own expense. The opportunististic band organizer takes the best of the partnership arrangement to begin with, then when the band earns income switches to the proprietorship arrangement under which the musician receives only an hourly wage or a lump sum. The musician is not entitled to verify the amount received, to see the bookkeeping, to criticize the expenditures, or to know what percentage of income he or she should have received.

The time to find out the exact intentions of the band regarding money is before joining it. "If I were to join, would I be a partner or an employee?" "If I am a partner, what percentage of the Net Income is mine?" "Who does the bookkeeping?" "When do I receive bookkeeping reports?" "How often do we evaluate the business as a group?" A few questions can prevent mistakes, misunderstandings, and outright fraud. Musicians who fail to get the position because they do

15

ask questions are probably better off without that band. If they are willing to work for next to nothing, they should volunteer for a good cause instead.

OUTSIDE ASSISTANCE

In the beginning, members of a band can handle songwriting, rehearsing, promoting the band, performing in gigs, answering phone calls, and so on. But when the band has steady engagements, its reputation has grown, and the members feel overworked, obtaining outside assistance may be the next move. When the band is ready for help, however, music agents are not always ready for the band.

Music agents become interested in musicians who prove they can support themselves with their music. Not having a day job means that the musician is committed, and playing in a band is not just something done on the side. Agents are interested in musicians who can come and go at the drop of a hat. If the agent says there is a job in Amarillo at 2:30 tomorrow, he doesn't want to hear, "Well, I've got to call my boss to see if he'll let me go." That usually means no job to conflict with a gig. The Los Angeles area is more flexible because it has so many actors and musicians demanding to pursue their chosen field. A bass player in Hollywood has a job with a publishing company that always lets him go. Flexibility is the agent's main interest before taking on a new band.

An agent's prime function at first is to schedule increasingly better bookings. A rule of thumb in one management company is that the band should be playing in established entertainment spots by the end of the first year. Agents advertise and keep the band's name before record companies; if a record company becomes interested they negotiate on the band's behalf. Agents have nothing to do with the production of records, but they do promote the band with recording intentions.

The main sphere of operation for agents is with live performances in clubs, resorts, and theaters. They have specific places that they book on a regular basis, and whatever bands they represent work in those places. One young musician worked one-night stands with an agent whose specialty was dance music for high schools, colleges, army bases, and weddings. The agent's type of operation is therefore a consideration when choosing and approaching someone to assist the band.

Most professional agents have been in the music business for many years and have influence with important people in entertainment. Inexperienced agents do not have such contacts unless they are affiliated with professional management companies. In that case, they work with mentors who guide them in the who and how of promoting bands. The band should ask various club and resort managers for opinions about agents before signing a contract. The consequences of being mismatched by an inexperienced agent was related by a guitarist: "I was in a jazz band that played an outdoor concert. After four or five songs everybody was screaming for rock'n'roll. One guy on a Harley rolled right up on the stage and demanded we play rock. Pretty soon rocks were flying by our heads."

A contract is signed to define what services the agent will provide, the fee for those services, and how long the services will continue. The commission is usually from 10 to 20 percent of gross earnings. The club pays the agent, who deducts the commission before paying the band. Sometimes the agent's extra expenses are also deducted. An agent may invest considerable time and money in a band before any return is realized. For that reason, contracts are for a minimum of two years, so that the initial investment is paid back. Who signs the contract for the band depends on the type of organization. In a proprietorship, only the business owner signs. In a partnership, all the partners sign.

A contract is a binding agreement that is enforceable in a court of law. Never sign a contract without understanding and agreeing with its terms. Never give an agent total power of attorney to sign papers for the band. And never give an agent any part of royalties on the band's original songs. The only ongoing interest an agent should have after expiration of a contract is in an album arranged with a recording company.

Joining a band is an important step in a musician's career. Careful examination of its business arrangements makes the difference in whether or not that step is profitable to a self-supporting musician.

FACTORS IN GOOD REHEARSALS

Individual rock musicians become an integrated rock band through rehearsal. It is here that cooperation between the musicians is developed down to the smallest musical detail. The object is to appear before an audience with a perfectly coordinated expression of the music. All band members must be present at rehearsals knowing exactly what they are to do. Tardiness, missing practice, or wasting time cannot be tolerated. A member who misses practice or a show is dismissed immediately, because the band is a group activity whose whole effort is dependent on full attendance. Musicians must accept this fact from the beginning, or they won't be in the business very long.

A site for rehearsal is usually found by the band manager with input from other members. They try to find a place that is convenient for all. In small cities or spread-out towns, it may be possible to practice in a home, if it is well insulated. Bass notes cut through walls like a hot knife through butter. The neighbors must consent, or the house must be distant enough not to bother them. Probably the best option is a basement with an insulated ceiling. The curfew in most states is 9 or 10 p.m., after which the police may be called for noise control.

In large cities, rehearsal is generally in a rented hall. The rent varies from $5 an hour up, with the cost advanced by the manager from the band's bank account. The account is reimbursed out of proceeds from the next performance. A rehearsal hall is advantageous because it is usually equipped with a large mirror on one wall. The band can observe themselves during practice to develop stage presence. Other places for rehearsal may be a church, school, or business that is closed for the night.

"We practiced in the same rehearsal hall for seven years," recalled one musician. "Our bass player owned it and lived in it, too. When we started, the place was just a shell, with curtains making the rooms. By the end he had built walls with soundproofing and had seven spaces to rent out. There was no problem with neighbors because the hall was in an industrial area, by a freeway, and under power lines. Whenever we played a gig, the owner was right there to collect the rent we owed him."

The smaller rehearsal room dictates lower volume for practice. Other advantages of lower volume are that it enables each member to hear what the others are playing, and it conserves energy for a long practice.

The instrumentalists and vocalists practice separately and are put together when both have been perfected. If a definite performance is coming up, the whole routine for the performance is rehearsed in one session. A cue sheet for the night is supplied to each member to ensure that everyone knows the order of songs to be played as if on stage. For each new performance, a different cue sheet is practiced, to explore the possibility of a better

A basement with insulated ceiling for band rehearsal keeps sound from irritating neighbors.

sequence and sound. The audience likes to hear familiar songs but not necessarily in the same order every week.

The number of songs the band prepares depends on the kind of audience. Dance bands should have four sets of songs. A set is composed of ten to fourteen songs and provides forty-five minutes of music. If the band is playing for a show, just one set is sufficient.

Finding an appropriate place to rehearse is a challenge every rock band has to overcome. The difficulty for a beginning band is paying the rent, unless a home can be found among the members. A young musician might persuade his or her parents to provide the space and put up with the noise. At least parents know where their teens are when they are practicing at home.

SONGWRITING

Identifying the songwriter is important, because publishing royalties are paid to that person or group. Writing a song can greatly augment the earning power of a musician if it is recorded and becomes a hit. It may be played on radio stations or by other performers, earning even more income for the writer.

There are no hard and fast rules for writing songs. Most composers try to do one song every day, no matter how bad it sounds at the time. They record their ideas on a tape recorder, or write on a notepad, or brainstorm with the band until an inspiration takes hold. One person may come to practice with the germ of an idea, and the whole band writes the song.

Whoever writes the musical part of the song, the melody, is referred to as the *composer*. Whoever writes the words is the *lyricist*. *Songwriter* refers to a person who writes both melody and words, although the terms are often used interchangeably.

Songwriting should not be confused with arranging. If band members enhance the song with their instruments, harmonizing with the melody, that is arranging. The song remains unchanged even though it is fuller and richer with various instrumental parts. Songs are copyrighted, but arrangements are not.

A frequent structure for a simple rock'n'roll tune is: verse 1, chorus, verse 2, chorus, bridge, verse 3, bridge, repeat verse 1 or 3. The bridge is a short passage, usually in the middle of a song, that links the verses and provides variation from the melody. It can be employed to modulate from one key to another. The chorus may be in a higher key to give a lift from the verses. In dance music, one chorus is repeated over and over in hypnotic rhythm. These are only guidelines; songwriters take many liberties in songwriting.

In the 1970s songs came to a deliberate stop, but now they fade away. The practical reason for the fade is to give radio stations discretion as to when a song ends and commercials begin. Timing is very important in radio, so the fade provides the necessary flexibility. Other than that, hard rock music still has hard endings, and dance music seems never to end. Three minutes is the average time for a song, since that is the time allowed for each song on radio. Not every song is written for radio use, but many songwriters have it in the back of their mind because of the royalty possibilities.

Creating music that has audience appeal is basic to popular music, including rock. To that end, it is helpful to get the opinions of several listeners. A study of music sales charts gives clues to what people are listening to at the moment. Music trends change over a ten-year period, and the middle of the decade seems to be the peak of a particular trend. Being completely original in music means not being popular. The listening public does not want anything radically different—just a little different. The cutting edge of original music may be too odd or strange for most listeners. To sell music, the band has to gear its efforts toward trends or being just ahead of them.

Radio stations acquire records from distribution centers, which are controlled by the major record companies. The media have no choice in the music they receive. The record companies are not interested in educating people or developing their tastes with avant-garde music. They are interested in making profits by selling music with a proven following. Radio stations play only what the listeners request, so record companies search out music to record that already is acceptable to the public.

Besides royalties, songwriters enter contests for prizes. Various societies, usually active near recording centers, sponsor songwriting festivals. They also sponsor seminars and classes on songwriting. Competitions offer the songwriter the chance to sharpen skills and to try out new ideas in music. Those that place in the contest catch the attention of music industry officials. Prizes can be substantial amounts of cash, so the winning songwriter stands to gain more than a personal victory.

Many bands do well playing Top 40 songs, which means popular but not original music. The potential for profit, though, is greater for the band that discovers a music trend a little ahead of its time. They or their songwriter create songs to appeal to that trend.

To prepare for a career in rock music, a teenage musician goes one step beyond practicing on an instrument. That step is to find other musicians to form a small band and learn how to work together. When musical cooperation has developed and the teen desires to make a career out of a hobby, the search for a professional band begins. This search is different, because the goal is to make

23

music a career to support independent living. Before joining a band, judgments must be made about leadership, income, outside help, and compatibility with band members and their music. Once the band is rehearsing, they may choose to create original music or to play new songs by writers within the group.

Eventually the day comes when the new band is happy with its rehearsal of songs and wants to be heard in public. Live performances bring new challenges, as we shall see in the next chapter.

2

Steps to Live Performance

TRAVEL ARRANGEMENTS

When the band is ready for performance before a live audience, the unglamorous but practical issue of how to get there presents itself. Travel is part of auditioning for work and performing in town and out of town. All the band members and all the instruments have to be moved and in place by a specified time.

Travel in town is usually arranged individually. Like a group of people going anywhere, members get there by themselves or prearrange rides with one another. If parking is likely to be a problem, the band members arrange to go in one vehicle with all the instruments. They may unload at the back door and need only one parking space.

Out-of-town travel is usually planned by the manager or by the group at his or her suggestion. The costs of travel and lodging are deducted as business expense from whatever income is made on the trip. Ideally, the band travels in a fully insured, dependable van with enough storage space for instruments and equipment. If the band begins to do a lot of traveling, a motor home offers the advantage of cutting down on hotel bills. It also provides the comfort of having your own bed, bath, and TV each night after work.

When a music agent finds an out-of-town engagement for a band, parking instructions are provided along with travel instructions. If a motor home is used, ordinary parking spaces won't do, and the agent must make other arrangements.

Well before departure time, the weather forecast needs to be checked for storms and the highway department for road conditions. One band was delayed by an unexpected blizzard. In the rush to set up the stage, a satchel containing money and personal belongings was dropped in the lobby. When they came back to retrieve it, it was gone. Everything they earned that evening only made up for the loss.

Ideally, the band member with the best driving record delivers the band without the delays of speeding tickets or accidents. Most of the time, everyone takes a turn driving so that no one person is worn out before the performance. They do not drive home the same night after an out-of-town gig. Falling asleep at the wheel is very dangerous. They either rent a room for the night or stay in the motor home. On longer tours, a driver may be hired so the band can catch up on sleep.

A manager with a strong sense of organization is very important to the smooth operation of a tour. Such a person saves time, trouble, and money for the whole group. A story of all the things that can go wrong was told by a drummer in a group about to go on tour.

"Our first show was scheduled in New York. We were in Los Angeles and planned to leave early in the morning in a previously owned van that the manager had just purchased from the border patrol. Musicians are night people, so when he arrived at six o'clock in the morning to pick me up first, I was hardly awake. Because we were in a large city, it took all morning to pick up the other band members. Then when the van was loaded with people and equipment, the manager remembered that he needed to put on new tires. So we were delayed for the afternoon while new tires were installed. It was nightfall before we finally headed out of town.

"I wish that was the end of the story of our troubles with a manager who wasn't organized, but it was only the beginning. Somewhere between Barstow and Needles, California, the van broke down. We could see the glimmer of lights up ahead, so all got out and pushed for what seemed like miles. The lights didn't get any closer. A couple of the guys decided to walk ahead to try to catch a ride while the rest of us stayed with the van. After a while a helicopter came over, circled, and landed nearby. A man in a uniform leaped out and asked if we were in an immigration van. I answered yes, but that a private party had just purchased it. With that he jumped back in the helicopter and flew off, with no offer to help.

"Shortly after, the walkers returned, not having reached their destination nor receiving any offers of rides. We figured our dreadlocks may have scared off some drivers. We sat out the rest of the night trying to sleep, which was no easy job on the side of a hill. We didn't see the manager leave at daybreak to try for a ride again, so we didn't know which way he had gone. Later in the day the police finally arrived. Apparently the spot where we broke down was between jurisdictions, so police cars seldom patrolled it. The officer sent out a tow truck from Needles, so we all went there. As it turned out, the manager had gone in the other direction, and when he returned with a tow truck we had vanished.

"We got the van repaired in Needles, then just waited until the manager found us. By that time we felt like we were in the Twilight Zone and had fallen into a pit with no way out. The manager did find us, and we persuaded him not to take any more chances with that van.

"He had not given up on New York, though. Back in

Los Angeles, we waited around while he found space for us on the airlines. Before we took off, we learned that all New York airports were closed because of some weather condition. When I called my roommate to pick me up, she couldn't imagine how I could have been gone three days and never have left California."

Whoever makes arrangements for the band's travel should be a group-minded person who plans ahead. It also helps to be a little pessimistic and anticipate problems before they happen.

PROMOTION OF THE BAND'S REPUTATION

To understand promotion, think of a farmer planting seeds, tending the plants as they grow, and harvesting a crop. Planting can be compared to practicing with your band. Harvesting can be compared to live performances or recordings resulting in paychecks. Tending the plants as they grow is promotion. The farmer must water, weed, and cultivate his crop. The band must stir up interest from the public, entertainment businesses, and recording companies. Even the biggest stars continue to promote or they lose their following.

The object of promotion is to enhance the band's reputation so that their services will be in demand. Knowing who wants rock music enables the band to tailor promotion in that direction. Ever since Alan Freed played African American rhythm and blues on a Cleveland, Ohio, radio station in 1954, white teenagers have been clamoring for more. Soon, Bill Haley, Chuck Berry, and Elvis Presley picked up the pronounced beat, and the style was renamed rock'n'roll. Over the years rock has absorbed exotic influences from cultures around the world, but it still retains its own distinctive sound and special appeal to youthful audiences.

The Mill Avenue Merchants Association in Tempe, Arizona, wished to attract shoppers for weekend evening shopping. When they sponsored several bands to entertain in the streets, they didn't realize the powerful attraction rock has for teens. Shoppers didn't show, but unsupervised teens came from all over the county. When trouble erupted, the merchants appealed to the city for ways to calm the crowds. Between the police and the city fathers, a plan was conceived to pipe in more mature music, such as Chopin concertos. The state's hottest teen hangout quickly cooled when live rock was replaced.

The attraction of youth to rock is related to the growing-up process. It would be cause for worry if teenagers did not look for freedom from the older generation. Each new generation shares an urge to independence, which is normal and natural. African American rhythm and blues also expressed this search for freedom. Although blacks were not slaves in 1954, they did not have the freedom of whites to live in dignity, to vote, to earn a living. The young identified with the music, and ever since entertainers from Little Richard to Prince have been giving them what they want to hear. Popular music entertains; it was not meant to educate.

Promoting a rock band, therefore, hinges on that band's ability to make music that appeals to the urge for independence. The urge is expressed in various ways. For example, many teens successfully make the transition to independent living without losing respect for others. The equivalent in gaining freedom for blacks is the nonviolent way of Martin Luther King. Other teens think independence cannot be won without declaring war on the world. The equivalent in the black struggle for freedom is the Black Panthers. Both viewpoints and everything in between have been expressed in rock music.

The band that strikes this universal chord of freedom

29

in music and performs well will acquire fans if they are heard. Sometimes that means playing free to a wider audience, such as a band competition or music in the park. Classmates, cousins, and teen friends are invited to attend, as they make the best audiences. A band is loved by classmates because they know the musicians personally and because of loyalty to their alma mater. These invited guests form the nucleus of a wider audience who may not have the personal reasons for being there. The beginning band finds every opportunity to perform before an audience, even without pay, for the purpose of gaining fans.

Not many club operators are willing to give a new band a chance, because they assume the band doesn't have a following. The band's salesperson calls on various clubs, resorts, restaurants, and theaters to sell them on the band's merits. The process is laborious, but it is the only way to break down the resistance of club operators. The salesperson presents evidence, described below, that the band is experienced in the art of entertainment and has a following of fans.

When a club operator is interested, he will want an audition before he does any hiring. The band chooses three songs to play that will show their best qualities in a very short time. The audition is the same as a job interview for any other kind of work. Not getting the job does not mean the band was awful, but it could mean that the club was looking for another style of music. Once a club operator does hire a band, he rehires them again and again. A band may work with him once a month in the beginning, twice a month, then several times a year.

The mistake of novices in the business is believing that playing in a club automatically brings an audience. The reverse is believed by the club operator, who is counting on the band to bring in new customers. The point is that the band must cultivate its fans with the same care it gives to creating and performing music. The same fans are being sought by hundreds of bands. Promotion helps those fans choose one band over another. Some ways of making new contacts and keeping old ones are fliers, followup mailing lists, and newspaper releases.

Fliers

Fliers are like posters but the size of notebook paper or smaller. Generally they are designed with black print on white or colored paper. Yellow and light orange paper seem to attract the most attention and to be legible from the greatest distance. Clearly printed on the flier are the date, time, and place of the band's next appearance. The least expensive way to duplicate the flier is by photocopy. If a photograph of the band is part of the design, it will have to be run off by a printer. Fliers can be placed on public bulletin boards and distributed wherever young people congregate. They can be hung on windshields, on the doors of singles apartment houses, or wherever young adults live. They can also be mailed to club operators and others helpful to music careers. An effective promotion, though expensive, is to mail postcards with the band's picture on one side. It is a sure way to put the band's face, name, and message onto some important person's desk.

Mailings

Some bands develop large mailing lists and send out a newsletter every month with times and places of their engagements. The list is compiled by asking for the names and addresses of those who attend their shows. The punk rock band 45 Grave, based in Los Angeles, had 3,500 names on their mailing list, and thousands came to their shows. They could afford to hire a professional mailing service to prepare and mail their news-letters. If the band does the work, the newsletter must be typed. It may feature articles on individual band members and fans, with pictures, cartoons, and want ads along with a listing of upcoming dates.

Press Releases

A newspaper article about the band is an excellent promotion. Advertising and the press release are two ways to get into the music press. Reporters have to fill their pages with news, so when bands submit articles they are helping reporters do their job. Besides the date, time, and place of the band's next appearance, the press release must feature some unique feature of the band. Does it specialize in a particular kind of rock music or lyrics? Perhaps it had an unusual experience while performing. The life-style and philosophy of the members can be explored. Never compare the band's music and style to another band, for copycats are not news-worthy. Several ideas should be written up and evaluated for grammar and spelling before submission to the newspaper. If the band is playing out of its usual area, complimentary tickets to the show should be given along with the press release.

Advertising

The other way to get into print, advertising, is effective but can be very expensive. A one-inch ad in the entertainment section is better than nothing, and it does keep the band's name before the public. The entertainment page in newspapers has been a very good device for local bands, which now get newspaper coverage that once was reserved for superstars coming through town. It creates an opportunity for new bands to reach larger audiences sooner.

Reducing the price of the ticket is one method of compiling a mailing list.

Press Kits

Operators of clubs or other entertainment places have to be convinced that a band has a following. A helpful tool for selling the band to these operators is the press kit, a collection of fliers, newsletters, press releases, and advertisements about the band. The kit should also contain evidence of where they have played and what kind of crowds they pull. Items of evidence are programs, after-event news stories, ticket sales results, and photographs of the band on stage and the audience. When starting out, the band should save everything. The best items showing career advancement are selected and artfully arranged in a notebook. It is updated periodically to include only the best evidence of a band's popularity. The press kit is worth the effort, for it opens the door to auditions. Through auditions, operators decide whether or not band styles are appropriate for their audiences. The press kit may just be the extra edge needed to get the job.

The Showcase

Another means of breaking down the resistance of club operators is the showcase. Bands perform in showcase clubs without pay, providing an opportunity to invite potential employers and whatever fans they may have to hear them in a clublike environment. The drawback is that many showcase clubs have sprung up in recent years. The operators take advantage of young talent by focusing more on selling food and drink to the audience that has been invited by the band, instead of providing favorable surroundings for the promotion of the band. The band must investigate the reputation of a showcase club before appearing, or it may do more harm than good.

Networking

The traditional place for musicians to meet has been professional organizations such as unions and guilds. They regularly hold seminars, meetings, and workshops where musicians congregate and get to know each other—a form of networking for individual musicians. Bands also may find work through recommendations of other union members. Rock music has stayed away from traditional organizations, because every community has its own form of rock network. Band members have to find it and start participating to keep those entertainment jobs coming in.

Since band business is usually conducted over the phone, it is not necessary to buy stationery with printed letterheads. The most important tool of a band is a telephone with a permanent number. An answering service or an answering machine catches all calls and enables callers to leave messages.

Rock'n'roll is a service that has to be sold to the fans by giving them music they want to hear rather than music they ought to hear. Beyond that, the combination of band and fans is a service that has to be sold to operators of entertainment places. They want to know if the band approaching them for work can draw a certain kind of audience. To convince them, the band prepares a press kit full of evidence of their popularity. Once upon a time, a band could succeed with no more than good music. Today, so many bands are seeking the attention of fans, and fans are fickle, so that keeping up on promotion is as important as the music.

ON-STAGE CONSIDERATIONS

The band's appearance begins with setting up the stage. Members arrive early for acoustic and lighting checks, then wait nearby until time for the performance. If another person is responsible for these adjustments, band members try to learn them in case of emergency. Sometimes substitutes are needed.

Band members are positioned on stage to hear the other members' parts. The bass guitar and drums lay the beat, so they are often placed at center stage rear. The rhythm guitar and keyboards are placed on opposite sides of the stage for a balanced stereo effect. The singer stands at center stage front, with the PA system on both sides. Amplifiers are angled slightly inward for stereo advantage.

The lights are placed to spotlight the band. If members are not present for the light check, they may have too much light in their eyes or glare from the instruments.

Some players have been horrified when their instrument did not sound the way it did in the rehearsal hall. The object of a sound check is to make the sound right out in front, not necessarily where the musician is standing. When everything is in place, the lights are adjusted, and the sound is right, the instruments are tuned.

A keyboardist in one band thought she had time to run an errand after the sound check and before the show was to begin. She came back in plenty of time, but no one answered the stage door. So many ticketholders were crowded around the building that she had to fight her way to the front entry. The doorman wouldn't let her in, no matter how she tried to tell him over the noise that she was in the band. Five minutes before showtime the owner happened by, saw her face pressed against the glass, and gave the order to let her in.

In another instance, the vocalist in a five-piece band was not so lucky. He rushed out after the checks to pick up his girlfriend, and it was four hours before he returned. The remaining band members were able to cover for him, but they worried through the whole

Members of U2 check the acoustics before a concert on their "Rattle and Hum" tour (AP/Wide World Photo).

performance. He had gotten stuck in a traffic jam on the freeway. It's best to stay right on location until the show is over.

Well-known bands are often preceded on stage by support bands. This gives exposure to lesser-known groups as well as practice in appearing before audiences. The support band starts on time regardless of the size of the audience. It may seem strange to play to an empty hall, but people are attracted to sound and soon appear.

At the last rehearsal, the band practices from a song list what is to be played at the next show. Each member carries that song list with him to the stage as a precaution against forgetting, which can happen during stage fright. The songs are grouped into sets, and they are ordered in certain ways to move the crowd to excitement or to reach a peak at the end. Slower tunes are placed next to faster tunes to create contrast. The set may be altered each week because the audience likes to hear familiar songs but not necessarily in the same order.

Band members do not talk to one another on stage, but they do have other means of communication. Little hand movements or facial expressions are agreed upon ahead of time as cues. They also help to focus attention in case of distraction, which can happen before a large audience.

The charisma of a band starts with the style of music. Their fans expect them to play rock, but inside the large framework of rock are many variations. Whatever that variation may be, the band should concentrate its energies on doing it well. To venture into other styles of music in one program is to confuse the audience. The only exception would be if the entertainment spot where they are performing specializes in Top 40 songs.

How a band arrives at its particular variety of rock begins with each musician's past learning experiences. When children begin to learn an instrument, too often they are only given exercises to develop finger skills. At the same time they should be doing games to discover new sounds and experimenting to invent new tunes. Through that balance of learning and expressing, musicians acquire the basics of their craft without losing their individuality. They grow up with confidence in their own musical expression because their trial-and-error ideas were accepted. They are not content with imitating other people's music and style. They search for that expression they will be comfortable playing. And because they are true to self, their musical style is as unique and personal as handwriting.

A particular variety of rock takes shape as the members integrate their parts into a whole during rehearsals. This means starting with a good song, because even the best performance will not improve a poor song. It means accommodating the vocalist. Whatever key the vocalist needs is the key for the instrumentalists. If it is too high or too low, the audience knows right away that something is wrong, for a straining vocalist cannot be disguised. If the tempo is too fast, the lyrics will not be understood. If it is too slow, the lyrics will drag and the audience will go to sleep. Even with the right song, key, and tempo, another intangible is still needed. In the business, it is called "feel" or "groove," and it has to do with every note and part coming together in the right way.

Once the band's unique style is identified, it can be enhanced by clothes, stage props, and the M.C.'s mannerisms. All work together for a total package, but that does not mean it is a contrived look. The band members already wear clothing styles that are extensions of their personalities as much as their music. A visual designer can enhance that style without changing its direction, and can emphasize the style for easier recognition. Sting's nail-studded leather jackets extend their metal rock, just as school clothes extend the charisma of New Kids on the Block.

Bruce Springsteen and the E Street Band have special appeal to America's workers. Their image grew out of childhood in a small community of factory workers. Springsteen wrote songs about situations he had been in, his hometown, and the people he knew. The blue-collar effect was increased in concert by wearing blue jeans and ordinary working clothes. The audiences came to the performance expecting to see this unity of style. Frequently they dress like the band, to identify with them and to say to the world, "This is the kind of person I am, too." In Madonna's case, her eclectic style turned into a fashion trend.

Important as clothes are, in the opinion of the business they cannot substitute for the attitude of the

Master of Ceremonies and the enthusiasm of the band. Attitudes are contagious. If the hall is run down and the acoustics are appalling, the band members never reveal their dissatisfaction to the audience. They play with the same energy and professionalism as if they were in Carnegie Hall. The M.C. looks directly at the audience and seems to be extending a personal welcome to each and every one. Along with music style, each musician and each prop plays a role in supporting the band's charisma.

It is possible for musicians to become bored after years of performing or if the music is not to their taste. Two young rockers played a one-time backup for the Coasters, Platters and Drifters, singers from the 1950s. The songs all seemed alike to them, and they were in danger of falling asleep. To keep awake, they brought a television set to watch a basketball game. They concealed it behind an amp so the audience couldn't see it, and they watched while playing and smiling at everyone. The tempo of rock is faster, so it is doubtful that such a distraction would be either necessary or workable today.

Different clubs cater to different kinds of audiences. Depending on where the band is playing, it is possible to predict what the audience will be like. For instance, in dance clubs not much attention is paid to the band as long as they play a dance beat. The people keep busy dancing and as a result are well behaved. Art galleries and museums cater to people who come to hear the music. They prefer original music, listen carefully, and are hard to please. Singles clubs are full of people looking for dates. They like to dance and usually want to hear whatever is the latest on radio. They aren't interested in original music, but prefer Top 40 replays. Cowboy clubs can be a physical challenge. Sometimes the operator installs a cage for the band, to protect them from audience activity.

Most clubs provide security for the band, so safety is not a consideration in this career. Occasionally a band may have to deal with a nuisance. A man stumbles up on stage, reaching over everyone to shake the drummer's hand. If it is in the middle of a song, the members let him wander around until they can gently guide him away. In that way the audience doesn't see the band members as spoilsports, and the incident becomes more entertainment than nuisance. At punk rock shows, some fellows like to leap up on the stage, then back into the audience without being caught by the bouncer. Given the nature of punk rock, it becomes a game between the audience and the bouncer and is part of the show rather than an interruption.

A band was playing in a large auditorium before 1,500 to 2,000 people when all of a sudden the police came up on both sides of the stage. They headed for the bass player first, chasing him all over the stage while he kept playing in time with the band. He didn't know what the police wanted, but they were sure making his job difficult. The audience roared, thinking it was part of the act. When the song ended and everyone had quieted down, it was announced that the fire marshal had come to see if too many tickets had been sold for the size of the building. Everybody without a seat had to leave. The band may be safe, but members of the audience have died when too many people have crowded into an oversold location. The fire marshal's concern is with safety for everyone.

Putting the show on tape is a good practice, even though the recording may not be professional. It enables the band to hear the order of the set objectively and identify possible problems in the performance. It is best not to play the tape back immediately, but to wait until later when it can be heard with fresh ears.

Putting a good performance together is a lot like

41

holding jumping beans in your hand. If the finger of management or the finger of promotion or the finger of stage presence is loose, they all jump out and run away. Performing for friends in school is simple by comparison. A teen band may gather in a home, jam around until a few songs develop, play for classmates, and become an immediate success. Behind the appearance of "having fun," entertainment in the adult world calls first for organization. A band without an organizer works under a handicap. Second, all members of the band work on gaining fans with the same enthusiasm they put into their music. Finally, the attitude, behavior, appearance, and music are all focused into a style to delight and entertain the audience. For the entertainers, it takes as much patience, responsibility, and discipline as any other career.

When the band's popularity grows and the members want to reach a larger audience, they may consider making recordings. Will they have to move to do that? Is the band strong enough to survive the sharks? Are they up to the huge jump in competition? The next chapter presents a step-by-step move into the exciting but imperfect recording business.

3

Competition for a Recording Contract

Producing a Demo

It is possible for a band to organize, write music, play it, and go directly to recording, without ever having performed in public. That is the primary aim of some groups, who would rather gamble all on the slim chance of a recording hit than work the daily grind of the entertainment industry. A record hit can bring instant wealth, but the odds are on the order of a crap shoot in Las Vegas. This chapter is written for those with the resources to take the risk and also for hard-working professional musicians: those who have successfully provided the service of music and who now want to reach larger audiences.

Before a record is submitted to the public, a distributing agency, such as a record company, must be convinced of the band's popular appeal. To impress the record company, the band must produce a *demo*, which is short for demonstration record. The demo is usually a cassette tape because it is convenient and easy to mail. Instead of seeking auditions, bands send demos to several recording companies or their agents.

A demo should be as good as it can be made from beginning to end. It should represent a finished product; many first records for a company are reprints of the demo tape. When a demo is unfinished or leaves too much to the imagination, the record company does not receive it well. Demos can be recorded at home, at a live performance, or in a studio. The better quality of recording in a studio is well worth the additional expense.

Recording Studios

To produce a good demo, the band first looks for a recording studio that rents time. Capitol Records, a major company, has four studios that can be rented, complete with engineer. Some small record companies also make their studios available. Independent recording studios exist for the sole purpose of renting facilities.

Studio B at A&M Records is every musician's dream. Special acoustical effects are achieved through a ceiling several stories high. The walls, which slope in at the top, are suspended from that height so that they give with the pressure of sound.

Most studio walls are padded or acoustically tiled to prevent reverberation. However, a room that is completely dead does not resonate sound, so the band has to use judgment in selecting a studio. Common furnishings are a wood floor, two wood walls, two acoustic walls, and an acoustic ceiling. The equipment available varies widely also. In considering studios, get the advice of other bands that have already used them.

Once a few recommended names have been collected, call the studio for information. How much do they charge per hour? Are there any hidden costs? Does the cost include the services of an engineer? Does the band bring its own multitrack tape? When it has been decided that a studio is within the band's price range, visit it to check out acoustics and the engineer. Knowing the engineer is very important, as they all have their own distinctive style of recording.

When the right studio has been located and the band is ready to sign an agreement, don't sign anything that binds the band to the studio. Agree to pay only for time in the studio. Avoid offers of free time in return for a percentage of your royalties if your music succeeds. Avoid offers of management in return for studio recommendations to a recording company.

Current rates for studios are between $60 and $240 per hour, so offers to reduce the rate are tempting but costly over time. On a small budget, it is best to have well-trained band members who know exactly what to do, and to get in and out quickly.

During most recording sessions, the equipment is in good working order, but on occasion there may be a problem. Be aware that the studio will not want to admit it. Be warned if the engineer rants and raves over the board or says certain sounds cannot be done. If the board is not working, the band is within its rights to ask for a reduction of price or return of their money.

For bookkeeping purposes, obtaining an invoice from the recording studio gives evidence of the band's expense. An invoice is an itemized statement of the services and supplies provided by the studio.

THE ENGINEER

A recording studio is divided into two areas: the studio where the musicians work, and the control room where the console, tape decks, and other recording equipment are located. The engineer is the person who runs all the mechanical devices required to produce sound recordings.

The engineer is responsible also for setting up the microphones, the instruments, and the positions of the musicians to achieve the best recording. The two areas of the studio are separated by double plate glass windows, so that both sides can see each other but no sound penetrates. Communication is made through microphones and speakers.

The engineer tells the musicians to turn the instrument down or up or adjust this or that to make the recording as clear as possible. Special care needs to be taken with the drums, because they can sound flat or canned. The desired effect is that of a wide open space like a stadium so there is little echo. To achieve this, the drums are placed next to a wall so that sound will be reflected. It can take an entire day just to tune the drums and place them right. An engineer has to know the drums well, because they provide the foundation sound for the other instuments.

Woven into his knowledge of sound and acoustics, the engineer has a style of his own that comes through on the finished recording. As he pushes buttons, dials, and switches while the musicians play, his way of doing it will be different from that of another engineer. It is that style the band must listen for and appraise according to the sound they want to achieve. A clearly recorded loud sound may not suit the band if what they want is a clear soft sound. The distinction between science and art needs to be made here: The engineer is the scientist, and the band members are the artists. The mistake a new and inexperienced band may make is to let the engineer take over and remake their music. They hire the engineer to do what they have decided to do as a group. Any wavering at this late date can only add to the band's costs in producing a demo.

The difference between engineer and musician can be summarized as follows: After completing a recording for a band, the engineer puts the record on an oscilloscope (which shows the visual pattern of electrical waves) and is excited by the clean pattern, indicating no noise. The musicians anxiously wait to hear what their demo sounds like.

Engineer Kerry Jackson works the sixteen-track board in his recording studio.

The Recording Process

The recording studio can estimate how many hours to set aside for a first demo, but it is only a ballpark figure. The time to go to a studio is when the songs have been created and rehearsed to everyone's satisfaction. Each band member should know which songs will be recorded and in what order. The artistic interpretation needs to be secure so that rehearsing in the studio can be minimized. But because the instruments will have a different sound there, it is preferable to have a practice run before the serious business of recording begins.

The multitrack recording machine records on 4, 8, 16, 24, or more sections of tape simultaneously. Unlike monaural recording, where all instruments are recorded on a single track, in multitrack each instrument is recorded separately. The advantage is that if the band chooses to change the volume of one instrument or erase another, it can be done without affecting the recording of other instruments. Most studios have 16-track recorders.

The rhythm instruments, drums or bass guitar, are the first to be recorded. They are followed by the sweetening instruments, lead guitar, keyboard, and synthesizers. The vocals are put down last, with the soloist preceding group vocals. These days drummers can put down their parts, leave the studio, and never hear the other instruments that follow. The guitarist listens to the drummer's part on the headset while making his or her addition. The sequence is continued until all the instruments are recorded. The various instruments can be recorded on separate days so long as they are in the right sequence.

The first problem most often encountered in a studio is a drummer whom nobody can follow. In rock'n' roll, the drummer has to have a steady metronome beat. If the beat wavers, the rhythm is lost, and the other

The drums are recorded first to lay the beat for other instruments in the band.

instrumentalists have to guess at what the change is going to be. The rhythm is the one predictable repeating element that holds the musical variations of the other parts together. Therefore, the drummer must dispense with flashy rhythms to maintain an accurate count.

The other chief problem is players' failure to listen to each other. Four people cannot bang away at their instruments trying to solo at every opening. Each band member may play his or her part perfectly but fail to integrate it with the other parts to form a song. If the music has been arranged before the band goes to the studio, each member will know his part and when to play it. Song arrangement can eliminate the second biggest problem in the recording studio.

Studio operators complain that new bands are unrehearsed, ask to repeat, and even write songs during the recording session. If the band is on a small budget, it is to their advantage to be prepared, as every delay drives up the cost. Record companies prefer bands that work within their studio time allowance.

If a band is well established and has money to burn, however, the recording studio is an ideal place to create music. There are so many new tools to experiment with, and if it doesn't work it can be erased. The Beatles owned their own recording studio, which undoubtedly helped to inspire the originality of their music in later years. In the beginning, they worked under the same restrictions as other bands trying to get a start.

Mixing and Dubs

Once the separate instruments and vocals have been recorded, mixing the tracks brings them all together to create a unified sound. The possible combinations are infinite. Mixing should be done on another day, when everyone involved is fresh. The process of recording is too tiring, especially on the engineer, to try to do both on the same day. The best results come from imagining yourself as a listener hearing the song for the first time.

The mixing can be done by the band, a designated person in the band, a producer, or the engineer. Some people in the business think that the engineer, who works with the equipment daily, can do the best job on the basic mix. Engineers do know the potentialities and limitations of their gear and probably do get speedier results. Then the beginning mix can be refined according to the artistry of the person in charge of the final interpretation. The expertise of one who knows the market for this band's type of music is needed here.

Satisfaction with the final mix has to do also with the kind of speakers the music will be heard through. Records mixed for big speakers do not sound right on car radio speakers. The recording is adjusted for the size of speaker that demos will be played through.

When everyone is happy with the mix, the parts are transferred from the multitrack machines to the monaural machines, which are standard tape recorders. The temptation here is to save money by producing master copies on home recording equipment. The tape will sound only as good as the worst piece of equipment. If the demo is to introduce the band to a recording company, all the masters should be professionally copied. The quality of professional recording is better preserved this way than through home recording systems. Furthermore, all the dubs should be made from the master.

When the demos are complete, be sure to take the master tape from the recording studio, as it is required to produce more demos if needed. As mentioned earlier, a record company may want to reproduce a demo without any changes. The master will cost about $100, but the band's best recording effort would be lost without it.

CONTACTING RECORD COMPANIES

Why not produce and sell records now that the master tape is in the band's possession? Producing records might be simple, but selling them is quite difficult because record companies control distribution. It is virtually impossible for an individual to sell records anywhere but at a swap meet or out of the back of a car. Bands are dependent on the companies for distribution of their records. Consequently, considerable effort must go into courting their favor.

In the old days, bands developed their craft before an audience and established a following of fans. They hoped to grow so popular that a record company would approach them. In large cities such as Los Angeles, New York, or London, a famous band may be spotted, but it doesn't always work that way. Many great bands in those cities have never been approached to record. By the same token, bands that never played a gig in their lives have gone straight to a company with their demo and been signed instantly. But it doesn't always work that way, either: Many bands have been turned down by record companies.

Demos are still the accepted way of promoting a band's music, although opinions vary regarding their effectiveness. The companies receive so many tapes that they are either not listened to or given brief attention. If the band is based in the same city, the recording company might go to see them perform, making their chances somewhat better than one tape in an ocean of tapes on the company desk. In any case, care must be taken in the presentation of the demo, because the competition is so stiff.

In search of a record deal, the rock group Bam Bam set up shop on a flat-bed truck and gave a concert under the windows of a midtown-Manhattan record company (AP/Wide World Photo).

Following are a few rules for sending a demo to a record company:

1. Put the band's name, address, and telephone number on the tape's label.
2. Put the same information on the tape cover.
3. Put in the package with the tape and cover a typewritten biography of the band giving the music played, the member's names and their instruments, the songwriter's name, a list of contests won, broadcasts, recordings, and good reviews. Emphasize the band's originality.
4. Include an 8″ × 10″ black-and-white glossy photograph of the band, with name, address, and telephone number on the back.

53

5. Include a stamped, self-addressed envelope.
6. Include a cover letter mentioning all the enclosed items, how long the band has been together, where their next appearance will be, and an invitation to see the band. Ask for comments and suggestions. Don't brag. A cover letter is necessary, or the package will be tossed. If it is written by an agent or a manager, a friend of the addressee, or another important person, use of that person's stationery may gain more attention.
7. Package everything in a padded envelope or small box with neatly typed or printed address and return address. It can be sent by the class of mail for audio recordings plus first-class postage for the letter.

Plan a day on the telephone to canvass record companies before sending demos to them. Companies are as diverse as magazines. They specialize in certain music styles, produce different kinds of recording devices, and sell through a variety of outlets. Screening the companies enables the band to find those most suitable to their music and the audience they hope to reach. Following are some questions to ask, along with information to help as a basis for judgment.

Do you manufacture records and distribute them? What are names of some of your records, and where can I find them? The purpose of these questions is to filter out investors who present themselves as record companies but in fact have no ties with any. By slick salesmanship and contracts that no one understands, they sign up every promising young band in town. The band gives them recording rights to their songs, but the investors are not obligated in any way to produce records. They are merely speculating that one of all the bands they sign up will become popular; then they will promote that band with a record company. In the mean-time, the other bands are prevented from approaching record companies with their songs because they gave their rights away to counterfeiters.

Do you specialize in a music style? Although rock accounts for half of the music recorded and sold in America, the other half specializes in black urban, country, classical, jazz, gospel, and others. The record companies have to be narrowed down to those that do rock; then the kind of rock has to be identified. If a punk rock band approached a company that produced hard rock, their demo would not be welcome. A composer/band leader wrote Detroit Rock songs. The speedy tempo of this music appeals to people who live in crowded, inner-city, solid-cement environments. Therefore he approached independent record companies all over the world that distribute to densely populated cities.

What kind of recording devices do you produce? Buyers have consistently favored cassette tapes in most recent years. Currently, compact discs are gaining rapidly, and black plastic records seem to be disappearing. The band will surely want a company that produces the kind of record devices people want to buy.

Where may buyers purchase your records? The neighborhood record store attracts the most buyers and seems to be gaining buyers with each year. About 25 percent of all records are sold through other retail stores, record clubs, and mail order. Because of the volume of records sold, these other outlets still account for millions in sales. The band trying to break into recording may find it easier to work with companies that sell through these lower-volume outlets.

To whom should we mail our demo? Properly packaged and addressed demos are most likely to get to the right person. The demo needs to be heard by the person authorized to make a decision about it; otherwise it may shuffle from desk to desk in the company. Having a person's name helps in keeping track of the demo and its progress.

Once the canvassing is complete, make a list of companies to which to send demos. Leave space beside each name to fill in the date it was sent and the response received on follow-up phone calls. When the demo has been received by a company, it takes between three and six weeks to process. It is all right to phone after three weeks to ask if anyone has had a chance to listen to it. Companies have been known to listen to demos while anxious band members waited on the phone. To keep things moving, send out ten demos at a time; as they come back, send them right out to other companies. In that way, someone will always be listening to your demo, and at the least the band's name will be promoted.

Record companies are easily irritated by silly mistakes like receiving reggae tapes when they produce only heavy metal, or receiving demos with no return address or phone number. A band's chances are small enough without adding carelessness to the cards stacked against them.

Musicians have been ingenious in figuring out ways to influence the favor of record companies. Some have made the rounds like salesmen going from door to door with a product, but many such attempts go unrewarded. Companies do not have time to talk to people when they are under pressure to listen to hundreds of demos. The industry depends more on hearing the music than on hearing sales pitches. Another device is finding a job with a record company in hope of being promoted from within. The industry is wary of that approach and has an unwritten rule that no one in the business can be contracted as an artist.

Despite their best efforts, the band may not receive any offers from the companies they approach. Then is the time to recheck comments of company spokesmen about the band's music. Was there a consistency to their criticisms? What in the music should be reworked? Is the demo up-to-date? Recording artists keep alert to the need for change when their careers grow cold. Paul Simon was successful in the '60s and '70s but did not do so well in the '80s. He made drastic changes in his "Graceland" album, and it revived his career. The record-buying public and trends in music are always changing. The challenge to both beginning and experienced popular musicians is to stay alert, flexible, and ever ready with new musical solutions.

Such times as these are low points in the morale of bands. They become vulnerable to offers that seem legitimate but are not. Billy Joel said in a television appearance, "The business is based on exploiting artists, not promoting artists. Over the years, musicians, who are not historically good businessmen—which is why they are musicians—give away pieces." The musicians, feeling not as capable as they once did, reach out for other ways to get inside the record company door. That is when opportunistic deals are hard to tell from authentic deals. The band can protect themselves by learning to read and understand contracts or agreements that are offered to them. Tips on how to read a contract are given in the section Evaluating Contracts (page 62).

Publishing Companies

An authentic offer may come from a publishing person or firm. Publishers are in the business of finding original songs and making them available for sale through sheet music and records. They have many contacts in the music industry and can pave the way to a positive reception from a record company. A reputable publisher will offer to advance money to the band to make a demo and pay musician expenses. Such an advance is recouped when the music starts to sell; it represents a long-term investment in the band. Unfortunately, publishing firms are as difficult to break into as record companies. The band can distinguish the "sharks" from the legitimate publishers because the sharks want the band to pay them. They require fees for their services instead of investing in the band. If the band has to pay them, it is because their tie with the industry is weak and ineffectual.

Pluggers

An offer may come from a *plugger*, a person who was once associated with a major publisher or record company and therefore has inside contacts. The band signs a contract giving him the right to sign them with a company, and if he succeeds he receives a share of the royalties. In other words, when the records sell, the plugger collects a percentage of income, which reduces the band's income. The contract is for a stated period of time, after which the rights revert to the band. An opportunist would either expect the band to pay him up front for his services, or he would tie up their rights indefinitely by not having a reversion clause in the contract.

Producers

An independent producer may offer to record a band or rework their demo master. He has a flair for music that gains company acceptance, and he believes he could do the same for them. He advances money to make a master tape and directs its production. He generally does have connections with a record company, so the records eventually become available for sale. But some producers take far too much of the band's earnings.

Before signing any contract, the band should investigate the producer's reputation. Find out what other artists he has worked with and how successful their records were. If he does turn out to be a big name, the band should let it be known that they have an offer. The herd mentality rules in the recording business, so a competitor might be inspired to make a better offer. The band's royalties will be reduced, but perhaps not as much. The contract should contain a reversion clause in case records are not made within a stated time.

Young musicians are awestruck and uninformed about the industry, so they fail to ask questions or insist on changes. The sharks fool them into signing away their rights, while giving them nothing in return. Sticking to the basics and improving the music is the better route.

INDEPENDENTS VS. MAJORS

The general understanding is that the record company will make recordings, sell them, and someday in the future send money to the musicians in exchange for their music. Surprises do arise when the musicians find out that it doesn't always work so neatly. They are less mystified if one company handles the entire process from producing the master tape to paying royalties. Recording deals become messy when many independent contractors or companies are involved in the process.

Some of those processes are: publishing registration, mechanical licensing, recording contract, production of the master tape, manufacture of copies, package design, artist promotion, sales licensing, distribution, collections, and royalty accounting. Whether a band plays Top 40 or its own music may change the process somewhat, but those steps generally describe the path to putting records on the store shelf.

Record companies are either major or independent

companies, the difference lying in the emphasis each places on various aspects of recording operations. Independents, or "indies," are more involved with producing, manufacturing, and promoting the band. They distribute and license to a lesser degree. The major companies, or majors, are more involved with distribution of records and licensing of broadcast stations. They produce, promote, and manufacture records, but those are not their strengths.

The two are loosely dependent on each other. While the indies search out new talent to record, the majors watch to see how the public responds. Then they invest in the music trends that prove to be most acceptable to the public. Enigma Records was a successful independent company. They made the first record of Motley Crew, a hard rock band, which sold well. A major company, observing Motley Crew's popularity, bought the recording rights from Enigma. The major then put their label on the exact same record and distributed it through their retail stores and broadcasting stations. It won triple platinum awards.

Independent companies tend to produce music that is more original, while majors aim for what most of the public responds to. Indies appeal to specialized interests. The punk rock era, when bands were having no success knocking on the doors of majors, was the beginning of the indies. What radio stations wanted to play and what the majors wanted to produce was not in tune with what many people wanted to hear. The music-buying public is huge and diverse, with many minority interests that were not being reached by the majors at that time. The opportunities for indies have remained. Anything new or different, too hard-edge for broadcasting, having controversial lyrics, or ethnic in nature is not handled by the majors.

Indies are more willing to take chances on new talent.

They will work with a band to perfect their master tapes to fit the type of sound the company is known for. Their engineer and producer will rework and sometimes rerecord the master provided by the band. Indies will design the record cover, photograph the band, and otherwise create and promote the band's image. The band eventually pays for these services; how much they pay and the manner of payment can be ferreted out of the contract.

The weakness of indies and the strength of the majors are their distribution systems. The "Big 6" corporate companies are CBS, RCA, Warner, Capitol, Polygram, and MCA. Run by legal experts and accountants, they were licensing retail outlets to sell and broadcasters to play their records long before indies appeared. They have the financial resources to supply sound-recording devices on a large scale. In charts of record sales, majors distribute the Top 100, so there is no disputing their success.

A major label assures a band's popular acceptance because of the distribution advantage. People buy what is in front of them; even if a record is slow-selling, it still sells in the millions because of exposure. After two or three records with a major, a band becomes established in the public's mind. They no longer have to work at full intensity on promotion but can give more time to their music.

The indies have to find markets outside the majors' control. The best source is foreign countries, where the demand for American records is high. A thousand records were sold within four hours after the release in London of "I KILL ME" by the Jeff Dahl Band on Triple XXX Records. The most promising markets for sale of independent records appear to be in the United Kingdom, France, Germany, and Japan.

Public radio stations in this country play indie records.

Seldom are they heard on commercial radio, as the majors dictate and deliver what those outlets can play. An example of public radio is KPFX in Texas and California, which broadcasts special-interest music such as opera, Old Western Hour, or whatever is not mainstream. These stations are generally located near colleges, as are independent record retail stores. Indies follow up on this type of market by advertising in teen magazines, college publications, and entertainment tabloids. They accept mail-order sales when there are no independent stores to represent them.

Musicians working with an independent company have more say in the production of the master. Not as many records have to be sold before they receive a financial return. This is because costs such as finishing the master, manufacturing, packaging, promotion, and registration are paid to the company first. Also, these costs are lower than with majors because the indies are smaller and have lower operating costs. Musicians also receive a higher share of income on sale of records through indies.

Majors offer the benefits of large departments and more comprehensive results to musicians, but benefits add to the cost. Many bands are successful but broke. Twice as many records have to sell before they realize a return, and the percentage of sales of records is lower.

Both indies and majors offer advances to bands that sign agreements with them. They forecast the sales of a band's records and pay out part of the band's share ahead of time. If the advance is not covered by the sale of records, the band must pay it back.

EVALUATING CONTRACTS

A company expresses an interest in a band by offering a contract. A contract, or agreement, states specifically what the band is expected to do in return for specific things the recording company will do. A contract need not be accepted by the band in the exact form it is offered. A band should never sign a contract they don't understand or agree with. They can be forced to comply with the contract they sign. There should be no hesitation to make changes and send it back to the company. Sometimes a contract goes back and forth several times before both sides agree on all the clauses. The meaning of *contract* is "to draw together." A third party may help the band and the company negotiate the changes until they draw together in agreement.

For difficult reading, contracts are in the same class as insurance policies. The band will find the excitement of a recording offer fading with the tedium of reading the contract. The easy way out is to go to a music attorney, but then the musicians fail to stretch their minds where they need stretching. Understanding the contract furthers their understanding of the music business. It is well worth the extra effort.

Start by dividing the clauses of the contract among members of the band. Each person then finds a quiet place with a dictionary, pencil, and paper. He or she begins by breaking down the first sentence in that clause into smaller sentences. Suppose the sentence reads, "All monies paid by us to you or on your behalf or to or on behalf of any person, firm, or corporation representing you, including but not limited to recording costs, other than artist and mechanical royalties, shall constitute advances recoupable from any sums payable under this agreement, unless we otherwise consent in writing." This long sentence—and most sentences are long in contracts—can be reduced to: "All money paid by the company to the band will be paid back. This includes money paid for recording costs, but not artist or mechanical royalties. The money paid may be to other persons or firms on your behalf. The debt will be paid from your royalties on records in this agreement. Any change must be in writing."

Use the dictionary to look up the meaning of words. Some words are trade jargon and are defined in the Glossary of this book. When all sentences have been deciphered, use two different colored highlight pens to identify the promises made by the band and those made by the company.

When all band members have completed their part of the contract, they meet to match up the promises. Conditions fulfilled by the band ought to be followed by an action from the company. For example, a contract reads, "You grant to us and/or our designees the perpetual, exclusive, worldwide right to manufacture, advertise, distribute, license, and sell copies of the records produced under this agreement." The band is expected to sign over all their recording rights to the company. Somewhere in the contract there ought to be a matching statement promising that the company will manufacture, advertise, distribute, license, and sell copies of the records.

In the sample contract in Appendix B, the matching statement is to assign those rights. Pretend Records does not promise to make records, only to pass those rights on to another company. If the band signs the contract to set a 10 percent royalty on the sale of records, Pretend Records will add perhaps 3 percent. Then they will sell the contract to another company for a total of 13 percent royalties. If they don't sell the contract, no records are made, and the band is stuck. Bands should be leery of deals like this.

Besides matching up promises, the band evaluates every expectation of them in the contract to see if they want to comply. They make every effort to understand the contract, and making judgments for themselves builds their knowledge of the business. If they do not argue for their rights before the contract is signed, they could be legally trapped in an unfair situation. Perhaps unfair contracts explain in part why rock bands have spit on their fans, attacked photographers, urinated in public, and offended the American public in numerous other ways this past year.

The contract in Appendix B has already been reduced to shorter sentences. It affords a good opportunity for aspiring young musicians to test their ability at matching up agreements.

A fair contract from a record company would be to produce and distribute two single records and an optional album. If the singles do not sell well, the album would not be pursued. A company releases about seven or eight new singles per week. Those that attract immediate interest are promoted still further, and the rest are ignored. Singles and albums sell well in other parts of the world, especially third-world countries.

New technology probably will change American contracts in the near future. The industry is switching over to compact discs, and the black plastic record is becoming ancient history. Companies like compact discs because they have high-quality sound and are difficult to copy. When tape cassettes came out, one person would buy a record and the whole neighborhood would copy it. That meant fewer sales for the record company. A compact disc recorder will be invented someday, but for now the CD has better sound quality, a sales advantage, and holds more music. First contracts are changing over to one CD, and the singles are being skipped.

Once a good contract is signed with a record company, the band can expect generally the same from either major or independent. The company may consist of one person who arranges with other contractors to process the recording, or it may be a giant company with many departments. The first company person the band meets is the Artist and Repertoire person, whose work may be compared to that of a talent scout.

THE ARTIST AND REPERTOIRE PERSON

Persons who hold this position must keep constantly in tune with the styles and trends of the music world. They scan the ratings charts so they know what is selling best at a particular time. They read current events, demographics, and history so they can forecast the direction of music in the near future. They are in contact with other people in the music business: the press, studios, club owners, and professional managers. With this body of knowledge and background, they are prepared to listen discerningly to the demos that are submitted to the company from all over the country. Part of their responsibility is to check through the hundreds of demos that arrive on their desks daily.

Because of the sheer numbers, they are inclined to listen first to demos referred to them by their contacts in the business. They listen to everything but, being human, pay more attention to the familiar. A band's name around town, or other demos, or fliers received earlier may jog their memory. They are influenced by personal taste, but they also recognize music that will sell.

Artist and Repertoire persons, or A&R as the title is abreviated, narrow down the choices before them by gathering information about the bands. They talk to the managers, visit live performances, and get the opinions of the club owners. Then once a week or once a month they meet with other A&Rs in the company to submit names and further narrow the choices. They listen to a demo, talk about the melody or lyrics, and determine the audience it is geared to. Only one or two bands are selected for development in a year.

Another aspect of the A&R job description is that of

company representative to the band. When the band needs to talk with the company, the A&R is the person they contact. Whatever the company needs to say to the band is expressed through the A&R. This person is the link between the two organizations.

A saxophonist related how his band negotiated through the A&R. "An Australian record company did a single of ours that was sold to kids in the Outback. We got letters saying, "I play your record ten times a day," so we pressured the A&R to do an album of us. He hesitated because he had never seen us in person, only heard our demo. So we told him about our concert the following week. The A&R got on a plane and came all the way from Australia to see us. They did the album."

Just after the contract is signed, a long period goes by when nothing seems to be happening. During this time the A&R is putting together a plan to give the new band exposure. He or she might organize a tour for another band with the new band as back-up. He'll go on the tour, make radio and television appearances to drum up interest, and distribute free tickets. The purpose is to develop a public image of the band as featured artists of the record company.

Another important person to the band is the producer, whose work can be compared to the manufacturer of a product in other lines of business.

THE PRODUCER

Producers are of two kinds: those associated with record companies and independent producers. To minimize confusion, we shall focus on the company producer, with parenthetical comments on how the independent producer may differ. The main responsibility of this person is the creative production of a master tape. Secondary responsibility may be coordination of the production of the copies, package design, and promotional videos. Producers are paid by flat fee and salary. (Independent producers look for a cut of the band's royalties, which is more costly to the band in the long run.)

The number one qualification for this position is access to money to pay the bills until the record is producing income. The cost of producing a record for a major label is estimated at about $200,000. A producer, the A&R, and the company have to be risk-takers with a lot of confidence in the band they plan to record. A producer who makes a mistake won't be around long, as chances to make another mistake of that size are few. (Independent producers do not have company funds to work with. Unless they are independently wealthy, they find investors. Besides having to pay back the money, they must also pay them interest. Every penny spent by the producer to make a record is eventually paid for by the band. Therefore, they need to be alert to the differences in producers and the costs they will incur.)

Another qualification for the producer is experience in the creative side of music such as a musician, songwriter, or engineer. Not that having these skills is essential for the producing position, but familiarity with the entire process is. Working in the business is the producer's on-the-job training.

Producers are responsible to the record company, and everyone else answers to them. They are the ones with the musical concept and the creative and technical know-how to bring it about. All the resources of the record company are at their disposal for putting their musical concept onto a master tape. Where they start depends on the band's development. They may add some musicians or vocalists and drop others. They may add songs and drop some that the band had chosen. They may alter song arrangements. They instruct the engineer which instrument to emphasize. The master will not be over- or under-produced, because they know when to stop. A good producer enhances the musical style already established by the band. (An independent producer may not work within that contraint.)

Sometimes a producer takes great liberties with a band's music. This is tough for musicians who feel secure in what they have created: Suddenly their opinions don't count. Signing with a record company does mean that a band loses its independence. The producer molds and shapes the band into a sound that is better adapted to the listening audience according to his concept. Sometimes a musician goes into the studio, tunes his instrument, plays his part, and leaves without knowing what the result will be after the producer's mixing, cutting, and splicing. He has no part in selecting songs, in arranging, or in artistic interpretation because the producer has made those decisions and can do them with his equipment. The musician who does not understand this is in for a lot of disappointment. Recording musicians have less artistic freedom than performing musicians, but how much depends on the kind of producer they have. Companies generally try to match producers who are compatible with the band.

Unfortunately, persons of questionable business ethics calling themselves producers have manipulated ambitious young musicians for personal gain. The Milli Vanilli scandal was not surprising to people in the industry. The technology has made it easier to bilk the musician out of just earnings. In this instance, the producer made a video of two good-looking young men dancing and singing in front of the camera. Then he dubbed in someone else's voice. The dubbed singer received a flat fee but was not entitled to a share of the royalties on the best-selling video. She feels that she is the real recording artist and is entitled to the greater payment for her work.

Another story of an unhappy relationship with a producer was told by Tony. In his early twenties, Tony went west to make it big in rock music. He joined a band leader/songwriter named Carlos, who was from his hometown. Soon a band was formed, and they were rehearsing regularly. Before they had played any gigs, they were "discovered" in the rehearsal hall by a producer from a major record company.

In Tony's words, "Harris, the producer, was really excited about us. He was there every time we practiced—brought people in to hear us. He took us to his company's recording studio to make a demo. From there he was going to take it to the board of directors, and he assured us that he could persuade them to sign us.

"At that point another producer, associated with a publishing company, approached Carlos with a supposedly better deal. He wined and dined Carlos, gave him gifts, and visited him every day until Carlos changed his mind. When Harris, the first producer, found out about Jake, the second producer, he was livid. 'How can you do this? Here I'm giving you everything! I'm laying a recording contract at your feet!' The keyboard player sided with Harris. He seemed to be the only one who knew what was going on; the rest of us had no idea what the fight was about. In the end Carlos went with Jake's offer, because by now he thought Jake was a good friend.

"Jake didn't know that he had to rerecord us because Harris had paid for our demo and he held the master tape. Before we made a new demo, the rehearsal hall was robbed. All the keyboard player's equipment, about $10,000 worth, was taken, but nothing else of value. Jake told the insurance company that it was his equipment because the band was now under his control. He collected the money while the keyboardist lost everything.

"Then Jake persuaded Carlos to hire a studio musician to fill in. This guy came to practice, and after a while he'd say, 'It's been twenty minutes—you owe me $60.' The same music was rerecorded, but the results were horrible. It didn't sound the same with businessmen running the show. It didn't sell, either. The band just died in a heap."

A producer's expertise can bridge the gap between a band's music and acceptance by the record-buying public. It's up to the band to avoid the producer whose vision is clouded by power and dollar signs.

OTHER DEPARTMENTS

After the recording session is finished and mixed, the master multitrack tape is sent to the company **vault** for safekeeping. Sometimes the company is pleased with the demo, sees no need to hold a new recording session, and acquires the master demo from the band for production. These original tapes are carefully filed by the vault manager, who will dispense them when production and release dates have been established.

The **production department** handles the actual making of the records just before the release date. They order the sleeves or labels, and the master comes out of the vault for pressing. They press a small number the first time to see how the record sells. More can be produced if the demand warrants. The cost of manufacture is small compared to other costs.

At the same time, the **marketing department** organizes an advertising schedule according to the release date. Posters, displays, ads, and other graphic materials are designed, subject to the approval of the band and record company officials.

The **publicity department** knows all the newspaper reporters and advises the band on how to handle interviews. The aim is to get the band on the front cover of one of the main music papers, particularly when a record is being released. Publicity begins as soon as the band signs with the company, and every effort is made to keep them in the public eye.

While the drawing, printing, and pressing are going on, the release date is coordinated with live performances, a promotion tour, and radio and TV appearances. A promotion tour usually includes an interview on the local D.J.'s radio show and an appearance at the local record store to sign autographs in every town on the tour. The publicity department must know all the key people in the media. The prime objective is to broadcast the record on radio, which probably will lead to TV appearances, which will then affect the charts.

The **sales department** then solicits orders from the record shops. Orders come in easily for established groups, but it takes more selling, promoting, publicity, and marketing before store managers are willing to break for a new group.

The **international department** tries to get records released in as many countries as possible. First, the company has to be licensed to sell in each country. The music charts of what is selling there must be studied. They have to ascertain how much promotion and media exposure are needed to launch a new act. Then tours are organized around the release date as is done in this country. The independent record companies have specialized in doing business with foreign countries and have been very successful.

Many young bands, newly signed with a label, sit back and let the ball drop, losing their one chance at success. They assume that once they have a contract the record company will cause the world to beat a path to their door. But in reality, that's when the hard work begins. The record company does all it can, but the bands have to keep pushing their music, too. They have to go on the road and play the little towns and empty stadiums to drum up fans. Guns 'N Roses toured for two years before their records climbed the sales charts.

According to panelists at a music industry conference, talent is only part of the music industry. A band can have the best sound in town, but their musical brilliance guarantees absolutely nothing. It's their business sense, or lack of it, that makes the difference. Longtime rock star Eddie Money claims that the college courses he took in Business Administration helped him think about the long-term aspects of a career in rock music. Young rockers don't need a college degree, but they do need two-track minds—one in music and one in business.

REWARDS TO THE BAND

The songwriter, the recording artist, and the musician are paid from different sources of income. Occasionally, the musician is both the recording artist and the songwriter on an album, or the songwriter is the recording artist. The positions can be mixed and matched in a variety of ways, but tracking the money starts with the positions, not the individuals. To minimize the confusion, let us examine each position and the source of its income.

The songwriter is in the most advantageous position because he makes money whether records sell or not. This advantage derives from the copyright laws of the United States. The law may seem foreign to the music business, but it is the songwriter's friend. Were it not for copyright laws protecting the fruits of their labors, they might never be paid.

The composer files a form with the Copyright Office of the Library of Congress to prove that he or she wrote a song poem. Registration makes it easier in a court of law if there is ever a problem. Send for Form PA by writing the Copyright Office, Library of Congress, Washington, DC 20559, or call the 24-hour hotline (202)287–9100. Forms can also be picked up at any U.S. Government Printing Office. When the forms are filled out, return them with one copy of the new work, whether song or lyric sheet or tape cassette, which stays with the Copyright Office. The fee is $10 for each separate work. However, the songwriter can save a few dollars by registering many songs on one cassette. Only one title, such as "Songs of Mary Jones," is permissible for the collection. After filing, the Office sends a certification notice to print on the work; it should read: Copyright (year) by (songwriter's name).

In the early twentieth century, copyright law was extended to include musical compositions, giving songwriters exclusive rights to the use of their work for twenty-eight years. In 1978, a new law protected a registered copyright for the life of the composer plus fifty years after his or her death. The copyright can be passed on to another person in a will. It is illegal to print copies or make recordings except with permission of the composer. After the time has expired, the work is no longer under copyright and is said to be in the "public domain." The Copyright Office acts as a central source of information on the status of songs for the entire music industry.

The songwriter may assign the copyright to a publisher. By doing so, he gives another person the right to print and sell his composition. The proceeds are then split fifty percent to each. The publisher obtains a registration certificate from the Library of Congress. Then his company produces and sells sheet music. Royalties are paid to the songwriter based on sheet music sales. If the copyrighted song is performed in public for profit, such as in a concert, performance fees are paid to the songwriter.

To make sound recordings of the work, the songwriter, publisher, and recording company agree by contract to a mechanical reproduction license. The recording company produces records, tapes, and compact discs. Mechanical fees are paid to the songwriter for each record sold. The Harry Fox Agency is the main organization for licensing, collection, and payment of mechanical fees.

If the copyrighted song on one of these devices is broadcast on radio, television, soundtrack, or motion picture, performance fees are paid to the composer. Musak and other companies piping music into commercial buildings contribute also to the composer's income. Each radio station keeps a record of the music it plays. Performing rights organizations representing songwriters and publishers take samples of broadcasts for figuring copyright fees. The principal agencies are the American Society of Composers, Authors, and Publishers (ASCAP) and Broadcast Music, Inc. (BMI). The process can be lengthy, but it can mean a lifelong source of income to the creative person.

For the duration of the copyright, if anyone uses the song without permission, the composer may sue the infringer for damages. Singer James Brown has filed a three-million-dollar suit in federal court accusing 20th-Century Fox and others of copyright infringement. "The Commitments," a movie about an Irish soul band, uses Brown's 1963 song, "Please, Please, Please." The suit also seeks to block the release of the movie as a home video, because Brown's music appears throughout the film without his consent.

The songwriter for the band has royalty rights, but often in rock music the entire band contributes something to each song. Therefore several songs will be registered as written by the entire band so the other musicians may receive copyright royalties as well. If the band wants to use someone else's music, the copyright department of the record company arranges for permission and pays the appropriate fees.

The recording artist is the person or group featured on a record. An entire band may be the recording artists, or the band leader or vocalist may be singled out as the only artist. Whoever is so designated receives the benefits from record sales. This type of income is referred to as artist royalties.

Depending on the contract made with the recording company, the artist can receive from 10 to 25 percent in royalties. Suppose an artist has a contract for 18 percent of record sales. A compact disc priced at $16 would first have 25 percent deducted to cover cost of packaging. That leaves $12, of which the artist would receive $2.25. Sometimes a company pays only on 85 percent of sales, setting aside 15 percent for defective records that are returned and free promotional goods. That CD may sell for a year before the artist begins to collect royalties. Every dime spent—paying for the producer, the engineer, promotional videos, musicians, personal advances—is his money, and it is paid back to the record company one CD sale at a time from his royalties. Only after all of these expenses have been "recouped" by the company does the artist receive royalties.

The company collects money from sales and every six months sends an accounting statement and a check for royalties, if any, to the artist. How soon the artist is able to collect royalties has to do with how much money the company spends up front to produce the record.

The musician on a recording is paid by hourly rate or lump sum. He does not collect publishing or sales royalties unless he helped to write songs or is included as recording artist with the band. If the musician belongs to the union, the scale pay is about $200 for the first three hours.

Many musicians uninformed about how the system works have been duped out of rightful earnings. An organist gave days of practice with a band for no pay, expecting to share in the royalties from sale of records. Then her band leader signed a contract as recording artist, cutting out all the instrumentalists. She ended up being paid only for time spent in the recording studio to make the master. She never received the royalties she was expecting, nor was she paid for the days spent in practice preparing for recording.

Musicians are naturally interested in the people who buy their records. What are they like? Where do they live? Why do they like my style of music? A musician may start out with self-expression, but eventually he wants to know who it is that cares enough about what he is doing to purchase his record.

Surprising to many is the fact that American records go all over the world. Europeans buy considerably more records than Americans. Many record companies, especially independents, bypass the local market and go straight to England, France, Germany, and elsewhere. In world sales, Europe ranks first, America second, and Asia a distant third. Half of the Asian sales are to Japanese. The knowledge that most records go around the world undoubtedly influences the creative thought behind contemporary songwriters. The album "Stand!" by Sly and the Family Stone, produced in the late sixties, stood for integration. The song "Everyday People" was a plea for tolerance regardless of race, sex, or wealth.

This description of record buyers includes buyers of all styles of music; however, half of all records sold in America are rock, so the information is still useful. More records are sold in the South than in any other part of the country; the fewest in the Northeast. People under thirty years of age buy twice as many records as people over thirty. This trend has continued for years, though speculation is that the aging of the "baby boomers" may change that. Men buy more records than women.[1] Adding these points together, the profile of the average record buyer is a young Southern male or a foreigner.

How the musician is paid for record sales at home or abroad is determined by the contract signed with the company. Whether the musician receives 10 percent, 25 percent, or anything at all depends on what was written in that contract before work with the company began. It is highly advisable that musicians retain their own music attorney to evaluate the contract before signing it. The courts have been known to break contracts if the musicians were not properly advised, but that means an expensive lawsuit. When choosing an attorney, look for one who represents artists only. Many work for both companies and artists, giving rise to the charge that they don't negotiate hard enough when representing the artist. The attorney who works for musicians has a specialty in music agreements and deals with record companies on behalf of the musician. He or she helps musicians understand the contractual relationships they may be entering and guides them to suitable agreements. Music attorneys are generally found in larger recording centers such as Los Angeles, New York, Chicago, and Nashville.

Concerts, copyrights, and mechanical reproductions multiply the incomes of a few musicians into astronomical figures. In 1987, *Forbes* magazine began to publish an annual list of the world's forty highest-paid

---

[1] *Inside the Recording Industry* (Washington, DC: Recording Industry Association of America, 1991).

performers. New Kids on the Block, a teenybopper group, came in No. 1, with estimated earnings of $115 million for 1990 and 1991. Other top-earning rock stars were Madonna with $63 million and Michael Jackson with $60 million. Considering the complexity of music royalties, these figures are believed by accountants to be educated guesses at best.

Since 1958, the record industry has been giving Gold Awards to performers whose records sell at least one million dollars based on one third of the suggested retail price. In 1975 the Platinum Award was given for record sales of two million dollars. In 1983 the Double Platinum Award was given for four million in sales, and the Triple Platinum Award for six million. The awards alone indicate the growing popularity of records as home entertainment.

National and international awards have been given to musicians for contributions to humanity. The Polar Music Prize of the Royal Swedish Academy is to be given every two years and is considered the largest in the music world. Former Beatle Paul McCartney received the first award for bringing popular music to all nations over the last thirty years.

Let's say our hypothetical band took the gamble and made a demo to send to record companies. They shopped around for a suitable studio, since studios and engineers vary widely. Each instrumentalist prepared ahead of time to do his part perfectly, to get in and out quickly. They paid for the master and the dubs, and they assembled businesslike packages to send to the record companies. They canvassed the companies by phone to eliminate counterfeits and otherwise unsuitable operations. They kept a record of where they sent tapes and followed up with phone calls in three weeks.

When their demo was rejected, they solicited suggestions from A&Rs and considered making changes. They were disappointed, but resisted offers from opportunists. When a contract was offered, they didn't sign it until they understood and agreed with every binding promise on themselves and the company.

The A&R arranged for the band to appear in concerts. A producer planned and completed a recording, which was distributed to retail stores and radio stations. The songwriter was the first to receive royalty checks for use of his copyright. The band received recording artist royalties when the records began to sell and expenses had been paid off.

Sometimes a record doesn't sell. How does a musician make ends meet while waiting for a record to sell or for the next booking? What does he do in the waiting time? How does he handle the lure of drugs, alcohol, junk foods, and laziness? The next chapter reveals how a musician can influence success or failure by life-style choices.

4

Life-styles of Musicians

The form of the rock music business today causes the life of a musician to develop certain patterns. Hours, income, and other conditions deeply affect the leisure time of a musician and his family. So the person interested in a career in rock music needs to gather information on life-style along with primary occupational facts. The term life-style, as used here, refers to personal development, organization of time and finances, location, and supporting relationships. It includes that part of the day that is not occupied by work, whether preparation, performance, recording, or business bookkeeping.

LEISURE HOURS

Entertainers work when the rest of the world plays. Recording artists may keep the Monday-to-Friday, 8-to-5 schedule of the average occupation, but when promoting an album they also work when the world plays. Performing musicians expect to work during evening hours and on weekends and holidays. Occasionally they play at a morning bar mitzvah or an afternoon wedding. When planning leisure time, the rule is to keep evenings, weekends, and holidays open for potential work.

The musician's calendar always schedules work on New Year's Eve, although he may not know where he will be working until the last week in December. That is the one date during the year professional musicians know they can work. They seldom work on Christmas, as most people think of that as a family day rather than a party day.

A musician plans the rest of his life around the remaining hours of mornings, afternoons, and weekdays. Sleep habits are adjusted to roughly 2 a.m. to 10 a.m. Band members agree on practice time somewhere between 10 a.m. and 10 p.m. Generally, rehearsal lasts about three hours and is done in the evening. Some bands want to practice more than others, so rehearsal time is variable.

A musician may not work every evening he keeps open on his calendar. Some of that time may be taken up with promotion, managing, or bookkeeping. The unpredictable nature of the business makes it difficult to estimate the amount of leisure. So the division between work and leisure is up to the musician. Those who do not discipline themselves to choose career goals before play meet an early downfall.

THE LEAN YEARS

Rock musicians begin their career by performing without pay at community and social functions. They benefit by building a name for themselves as instrumentalists. When they become part of a band, they may find low-paying work in a club. Depending on the fans the band attracts, larger clubs pay more. As their following grows, they generate longer bookings in better clubs with increasing income.

In the beginning, money from music is scanty. The musician has to find a second job to cover living expenses. Because of the time conflict, entry-level positions are usually the only jobs open to him, and those are low-paying also.

A good part-time job for a musician is in the restaurant business: flexible hours, not physically dangerous, and generally very good wages (AP/Wide World Photo).

A good part-time position for the aspiring musician is as salesman in a music store. One guitarist found an advantage in meeting other musicians who came into the store to buy parts for their instruments. She had moved to a new community, so it was an opportunity to begin networking and building her reputation in music. She was paid not by the hour but by commission on whatever she sold. Some buyers drove very hard bargains. One man came in to buy guitars to resell in Japan. The store's price was $2,000 and he could make a profit by selling for $5,000. This customer haggled for ten hours, whittling the price down until there was no room for the salesman's commission. Music store sales is an excellent way to earn extra money, but only if the musician also knows how to sell.

Construction opportunities are plentiful, but musicians find them too exhausting. Lifting drywall and holding it up for someone else to nail to the studs takes strength. By the end of the day, the instrumentalist is too tired to hold or move his instrument. If a wrist or shoulder is wrenched, he may not perform for several days. Instrumentalists must be very careful of their hands because it is the precision work of their hands that sets them apart as musicians. Therefore, construction work is not recommended as a second job.

Restaurants that specialize in lunchtime meals fit within the time and safety boundaries of the musician. Late morning and afternoon work leaves him free in the evenings and early mornings. Work as busboy, dishwasher, waiter, or cook is not hazardous to the musician's ability to play. Waiters have the advantage in pay because they also receive tips. Before going to work for a restaurant, it is advisable to question whether the waiters share tips with the busboys.

Temporary help agencies are another option if the musician has transportation to work in a different place every day. Some have found good permanent positions through temporary assignments. The first years are tough years for the musician, so a second job is a necessity.

At the same time, housing, food, and transportation must be cut to minimum. Sometimes band members live together in a house. Space may be cramped, but everyone saves on rent. By combining resources, musicians can afford an area where crime is not a problem and houses are in good condition. Also, rehearsals are more convenient and less expensive if the band can practice at home. Care must be taken, though, to choose a house far enough away from neighbors who might object to noise.

Inexpensive apartments are available for the musician who prefers to live alone or in a relationship. Along with low rent, he or she needs a quiet location because of the need for sleep during the day. A young musician lived in an apartment house in which all the units faced a center pool. One day a couple began a fight that erupted into the pool area. They threw lawn chairs at each other and through apartment windows. Another neighbor, a Vietnam veteran who had a gun collection, stepped out to see what was wrong. In the struggle that followed, a man was shot to death. The musician gave up trying to sleep that day.

A week later, he was awakened one morning by the smell of smoke. He leaped out of bed onto a hot floor, grabbed some clothes, and ran out the door. A neighbor who had escaped before him saw her cat run into his apartment and begged him to save it. Going back through the smoke, he finally found a cat that did not want to be saved. It sank its claws into his chest and clung until the woman pulled it loose. By the time the firetrucks left and his wounds were bandaged, there was no more sleep that day, either.

For the next week the building was without electricity, hot water, or heat. He survived by getting an ice chest to keep food cool, and a friend lent him a battery-operated television set so he had entertainment and a little light in the evening. When a musician is young and ambitious, the hardships don't seem so bad, but he would have been better off if he had looked for a place that was quiet as well as cheap.

Money from music is also irregular. Like an actor, the musician may find longer bookings, but permanent positions are very few. Therefore, he must be able to save when he does earn to pay expenses when he does not. The recording artist who earns thousands of dollars on one record may not have another hit for years. High income for two months does not average out to much over a year. As a result, the musician spends a large share of his time in two tasks, finding work and planning his expenses between jobs.

HOME BASE

Work for musicians is found throughout the country; however, more opportunities are found in the larger cities. Chief among larger cities are those with big recording industries, such as Los Angeles, Nashville, and New York. Every band in every city competes with other bands for audiences. When they can do no better in one place, they move to wherever larger audiences can be found. Many bands and musicians have stepped up until they reached Los Angeles. The competition is now so intense there that bands are paying clubs to let them play. The heavy metal spoof Spinal Tap ran a one-day advertisement for a drummer in two trade newspapers, and 400 drummers responded. More opportunities for the musician do exist in larger cities, but the competition for those jobs is very great.

As a result, club operators and recording companies

know they can always find a replacement if a musician or band will not meet their demands. Seldom is a band hired for more than a one-time engagement. No two days in a musician's life are alike. He may play one day at a wedding, the next day in a nightclub, next in a TV studio, and next in a huge dance arena. No two engagements are in the same place, and possibly not in the same town.

The musician considers these facts when he chooses a place to live. If he thrives on competition, the challenge of the larger cities won't bother him. Smaller towns have fewer musicians to compete with, but jobs are fewer, too. Neither location has an advantage for the person hoping to be discovered by a recording company. A&R people are attracted first to sounds, so demos and pictures of the band can be sent to them from any part of the country. Home base can be wherever the instrumentalist finds other musicians to form a band and wherever he feels most comfortable with the level of competition.

The location needs of a songwriter are different. Being in the center of musical activity, such as near the recording industry, may be helpful for some songwriters. The work of others inspires their own creative energies. They are also in a position to learn first about new directions in musical style. But not all songwriters need this kind of stimulation, instead taking their cues from within themselves. This kind of songwriter could live on a mountain top and still produce. The songwriter may also be inspired by a unique environment. REM is a popular band from the Georgia countryside whose songs are peaceful, friendly reflections of the community they live in. For the songwriter, home may be wherever he finds his best inspiration.

After choosing a city, the next decision is to find a place in that city to set up residence. It is useful to locate near a freeway. Others prefer to live near the rehearsal hall or in the same area as other band members. The musician who takes time to plan will save needless travel and gasoline expense.

SUPPORTING RELATIONSHIPS

Living with a friend, partner, spouse, or other significant person is a beneficial relationship for the musician, especially during the lean years. If anyone needs a constant renewal of hope, it is a musician who is trying to become established. He needs to be reassured when uncertain, comforted when down, inspired when there is no vision. Some other person who understands and cares can supply what a musician at times cannot do for himself.

Anyone considering an alliance with a musician needs to be informed about the hardships. A relationship may not survive if the disappointments and delays come as a surprise. One woman tells of falling in love with the glamour of seeing her boyfriend on stage, with audiences giving him all their attention. It was exciting to be the girlfriend of someone so popular. But his fame was short-lived, and when his popularity faded, so did her love. She didn't have the big picture of a musician's life that includes up and down times.

Another musician's boyfriend left her because he was jealous of men in the band. Relationships have broken up over lack of money, especially when the female wants to have children.

The musician needs a partner who can see the positive side when bookings are not forthcoming. One fellow, who managed his wife's career as a vocalist, kept expenses down by eating oatmeal for a month. When his ulcer gradually went away, he learned that oatmeal is good for that ailment. The tough beginning years meant that they had to ration food, and he says those were the only years when they kept slim, trim figures without a battle. He knew the secret of keeping hope alive in a business that can be depressing at times.

Besides one close person, the rock musician needs a network of friends. If his partner becomes ill or leaves, the kindness of friends can fill the gap. They are a help in any kind of emergency, like fixing a flat tire when the band is waiting on the other side of town. Baby-sitting services are traded; meals are supplied when illness strikes. Friends share relaxing social occasions such as a backyard barbecue. These are not the kind of contacts that a musician networks for the sake of his career. Friends have other occupations and interests that help broaden the musician's concept of the world apart from rock music. The musician with a partner and a social network of friends is a strong contender in the business of rock music.

HEALTH AND APPEARANCE

The rigors of life as a musician require good health and energy. Performing on an instrument is a physical activity that lasts several hours. The instruments, furniture, microphones, and speakers have to be moved to the site of each new booking. Then they have to be dismantled, transferred to a vehicle for transportation, and transferred again to the rehearsal location. On tour, the musician must be healthy and flexible enough to adapt to a different bed and food in each town. Diet restrictions or back problems can be handicaps. For a musician to be sick means that he and possibly the whole band is out of business. Therefore, preventive health measures must become part of his life-style.

Musicians build endurance and strength by jogging and weight lifting. They eat diets low in fried foods and other fats that may clog arteries. Carbohydrates such as breads, fruits, and vegetables supply energy. Protein

Musicians set aside time in their daily schedules to maintain health and appearance (AP/Wide World Photo).

found in meat, dairy products, and beans rebuilds the body after injury and keeps muscles strong. They drink eight glasses of water each day. They sleep seven to eight hours each night.

Between the physical stresses of performances, musicians are tempted to spend free time watching TV. They are tempted to eat junk foods instead of preparing nutritious meals. They drink pop and smoke cigarettes out of habit. They cheat on sleeping hours. At work, they are repeatedly exposed to the temptations of alcohol and drugs. Persons who indulge in this way of life are not at their physical best. Their energy gradually drains away, sickness replaces health, and they are not able to meet the obligations expected of musicians. The effects of malnutrition, drug and alcohol indulgence, and inactivity do not show up right away. Musicians have to be aware of future health and energy outcomes.

It seems that every year we hear of the untimely death of a rock star from an overdose of drugs. The psychological stress of continuous competition undoubtedly takes its toll. Drugs and alcohol are available in places of entertainment, so the musician is especially vulnerable to addiction. Other musicians have the strength of character to avoid these destructive elements. Rock'n'roller Ted Nugent gave an antidrug message to onlookers while his crew set up stage for a concert. "Only you can help you," he said. "You have to love life, respect yourself, and want to see tomorrow. With those kinds of values you'll help yourself. No one can do it for you."

A healthy life-style or lack of it also affects appearance. Young men and women like to see other young men and women on stage who exemplify their physical ideals. That may seem like a strange statement after years of seeing rock stars with knee-length beards, electrified hair, warpaint, torn clothes, and other offbeat attire. The distinction has to be made between the costume the musician wears on stage and his bodily condition. The costume is part of the band's charisma carefully coordinated with music, body language, and stage props to create a unified effect. This effect is what the audience come to experience; they expect a certain assembled look to go with the concert. It may be the Latin charisma of Gloria Estefan and the Miami Sound Machine, or it may be the androgenous charisma of Michael Jackson. Boy George dressed like a girl on stage, but underneath he was a well-muscled young man.

The audience responds to both costume and bodily appearance. Though absurd costumes may be to their liking, weak and overweight musicians are not. Consequently, musicians are on continuous watch for potbellies, wide hips, and double chins. They have to be detectives to determine what irritants may be causing acne or cold sores. They check for bags under the eyes and other signs of declining health and appearance.

Aspiring rock stars may not be famous in the beginning, but they are still recognized and judged by potential fans as they shop in stores, eat in restaurants, or play tennis. Hollywood stars and starlets are careful about being photographed in public places because the results may be unflattering. Neither do they have control over where those candids may turn up. In like manner, the musician remembers that he has chosen life in a glass house, and he needs to be aware of his fans' interest in his life at all times. They do respond to the musician's general appearance when not in costume. Therefore the musician sets aside time in his daily schedule to maintain health and appearance.

STAGE PRESENCE

One way to acquire the grace needed for stage work is to think about someone in the audience and why he or she is present. Audiences seek entertainment to change the pace of work, school, and other trying circumstances. To entertain means to hold attention, interest, to divert or amuse. When someone in the audience sees an uptight person on the stage, he is not interested, diverted, or amused. Something in stage work is needed beyond the music.

Musicians are not actors, but both are in the entertainment field. The world has become seasoned in its judgment of entertainers because of television and motion pictures. They watch actors build their characters through words, facial expression, and body language. Those same viewers also expect to receive character messages from bands on stage. Bands have built on that expectation with themes such as Halloween spooks in Alice Cooper. Music, apparel, stage props, facial expressions, and body language coordinate to express a band's character.

The audience receives a character message from the posture of each band member. Slouching suggests sluggishness and dimwittedness, whereas standing straight suggests alertness. Leaning back on the heels suggests fear of the audience, whereas leaning forward on the toes expresses confidence. Hunched shoulders signal timidity, but shoulders down signal ease. Arms crossed in front are unfriendly, whereas open arms are friendly. Thus, band members can control character messages by knowledge and selective use of body language.

The band spokesman receives most of the audience attention, so he must be sure he talks to the audience, not to the floor. His eyes scan the back rows of the audience, for then he creates the illusion of giving attention to the front row also. He breathes deeply to prevent a wavery, nervous sound in his voice. He repeats the message several times in several ways so that all the audience hears it. The band spokesman learns from public speakers and actors how to do his job well.

Musicians have to be comfortable working in front of people. It is one thing to develop instrumental skills in the privacy of one's home and another to climb on a stage and display those skills before others. Weak knees, queasy stomach, and dripping brow do not contribute to good music or an entertaining experience. Aspiring musicians seek out public appearance opportunities such as acting in plays, making speeches, and performing on their instruments. It is only through practice before others that fear melts away. Stage presence is yet another skill musicians find time to work on during their free time.

The musicians of our imaginary band live in separate houses, but their lives are similar because of the requirements and conditions of the business. They found that they had to govern their leisure hours and not let them slip away. Sleeping from 2 a.m. to 10 a.m. allowed time for a second job, which was necessary to supplement income in the beginning. When they didn't play a gig, they rehearsed during those hours or did bookkeeping, promotion, managing, or some other music business.

During the lean years, they lived frugally and learned to spread their money out between gigs. Supportive partners and friends were an encouragement when business was slow. They disciplined themselves to keep healthy, good-looking, and aware of their fans when out in public. They worked at improving stage presence to be better entertainers.

This band is giving all they've got to stay in the business they love. Will they have to skimp and save forever? How will they climb the ladder to steady work, regional celebrity, or superstardom? Is being a woman or a minority a handicap? If all else fails, what can they do with rock music work experience? Statistics from the federal government may help in the search for answers.

5

The Job Market in Rock

The rock musician seldom plays alone. A single guitarist may play folk music, but the rhythm of rock requires percussion instruments. This style of music depends on drums to provide a strong, regular beat for guitars and keyboard. Therefore, the instrumentalist must become part of a group of musicians known as a band.

Chapter 1 described in detail how an instrumentalist looks for job openings in bands. The openings are for musicians who have developed skill on their instrument and have experience with other rock bands. Perhaps that experience was gained without pay in a student group, but it is necessary training for becoming a paid musician. The more the musician has played with various bands, the better prepared he or she is to look for work in the rock job market.

Musicians find job openings mostly through networking. Some may be found in newspaper want ads, music store bulletin boards, and temporary musician services. When a musician has reached the point of earning a living from music without working a second job, music agents become interested. Sometimes agents pair up various instrumentalists to create new bands that would be suitable for their stable of entertainment places.

Classified ads contain different types of openings, so the musician must use judgment about making a good match. Beginning bands are looking for beginning musicians. Intermediate bands may have a variety of purposes; some intend to stay part time; others may play a few gigs but hope for more. Still others only make recording demos and do not perform for live audiences. The advanced bands have large followings of fans who come to see them wherever they play. They have more bookings because of the crowds they pull to concerts, clubs, and so on. They look for advanced musicians, and they seldom need to resort to ads to find them.

If the musician is looking for a band that intends to produce demos for recording, other questions need to be asked. Is the ad for a backup musician for a soloist, such as Prince, or is it for a recording artist, such as each musician in Nirvana? The difference makes a big difference in pay.

JOB FORECAST

In a given day, an estimated 190,000 musicians go to work somewhere in the United States.[1] That does not mean eight hours of work, for musicians often appear for just one hour. Nor does it mean that the same musicians will be employed again the next day. Bookings are sometimes days and weeks apart. Rock musicians are only part of the total jobs reported here; others are classical musicians, vocalists, and other types of popular music. But the figure does help, in comparison with other careers, to judge the potential for finding work. Jobs in music are scarce. Students must judge for themselves whether they have the ability, desire, and competitive drive to enter that market.

During the '90s the job market for musicians is

---

[1] *Encyclopedia of Career and Vocational Guidance*, Vol II, William E. Hopke, ed. in chief (Chicago: J.G. Ferguson Publishing Co., 1990).

estimated to grow at the same rate the nation grows.[2] The musicians who work in popular music can expect slightly more growth, while classical musicians may expect less. This forecast is based on the expected increase in income spent on leisure activities. At this writing, our country is at an economic low, so the increase has not yet occurred. As one musician said, "Places where musicians play are disappearing about as fast as buffalo." People without jobs have traded live entertainment outside of the home for videos and cable television in the home. The club operators then turn to records and music machines instead of live entertainment.

Even the superstars have not been immune to the recession. Complaints by the North American Concert Promoters Association reveal how the entertainment industry is feeling the squeeze. Sixty percent of the acts on the road lost money for the promoters during 1991. They blamed the recession, high ticket prices, and poor quality of the shows.

THE COMPETITIVE EDGE

A rock musician does not need formal training or degrees, so large numbers of people do apply for openings. To succeed, therefore, the musician has to know the way around in the music business and be more ambitious than the average person. If job-seekers are skilled and experienced but still not finding work with a band, they need to broaden their search. They can still use their instrumental skills, though not in the first choice of entertainment.

---

[2] *Occupational Outlook Hardbook* (Washington, DC: Bureau of Labor Statistics, U.S. Department of Labor, 1990).

First, the musician must locate positions unknown to other applicants. Reference books in the library can serve as a guide to other businesses where musicians find work. The *Standard Occupational Classification Manual*[3] is compiled by the United States Department of Commerce. Every occupation listed in the manual has a number. For instrumentalists, including tuba players and violinists as well as guitarists and drummers, the number is 133 152041010. The number for vocalists is separate.

The next type of reference book is a listing of all the companies engaged in one kind of business. An example is the *Standard Directory of Advertising Agencies*, which contains information on 6,500 advertising agencies and is published three times a year. Each agency's listing includes classification numbers it regularly employs. The musician searches the listings in his or her area for the instrumentalist's number. Other business books about entertainment, radio, television, and recording companies may provide leads. Some states publish reference books about all companies in their area, such as the *Arizona Business Directory*. In these books, information is arranged by subject so that job-hunters may turn directly to the type of company that interests them.

While applicants make lists of companies that hire instrumentalists, they also should take notes on the companies. Such information helps in deciding where to apply first and make extra effort. It is also useful in making the résumé and press kit fit company needs. An advertising agency catering to baby stores will need

---

[3] *Standard Occupational Classification Manual* (Washington, DC: Office of Federal Statistics Policy and Standards, U.S. Department of Commerce, 1990).

different music from an agency that caters to appliance stores.

A copywriter in the advertising business once said that the people who applied for work with her often inspired her ads. In one instance, a certain drumbeat seemed to match up with one of her clients, so she put the two together for a radio spot. The applicant who has this information ahead of time has the competitive edge.

Job-hunters then canvass every company on the list. By telephone, they ask if the company is interested in one musician or an entire band. They ask for the name of the person who hears auditions, and they ask for an appointment. Doing spots for advertising or background music may not be the most exciting work to a rock musician, but compared with a job as part-time waiter, there is much to be said for it. It pays well and provides broad work experience in music. It adds to the musician's résumé and press kit, while building a dependable reputation. It opens the door to other leads in music. Just two or three companies that give temporary work could keep musicians busy in music, even though it is not rock. When the job market for live rock'n'roll opens up again, they can prove they have kept their skills alive, well, and ready to go.

ADVANCEMENT

Rock'n'roll has a Hall of Fame. Five hundred music industry officials vote to honor outstanding musicians for their contributions to the development of the art. The awards have been given each year since 1985, and a museum to honor the inductees is expected to be built in Cleveland, Ohio. Musicians are not eligible until twenty-five years after their first recording. The most recent awards went to seven acts that probably would have been named sooner if they had met the time requirement.

Jimi Hendrix Experience is at the top of the list for drastic changes in use of instruments. Hendrix performed in a mixed ethnic group with two British musicians. They were experimenters with sound, and Hendrix in particular opened horizons for guitarists to come.

The Yardbirds were a British band whose influence was greater than its financial success. Their records are now collectors' items.

In the 1950s Johnny Cash's music was somewhat rockabilly like Elvis Presley. Since that time Cash has leaned more to country, but the mid-'50s hit "I Walk the Line" is regarded as rock.

The Isley Brothers, Ronald, Rudoph, and O'Kelly, were a gospel trio in Ohio. In 1957 they moved to New York and began singing more secular music. In twenty years they recorded nearly fifty hits.

The music of Bobby "Blue" Bland has been called masterworks of rhythm'n'blues. He began his career in the 1940s and recorded sixty-three hits.

Two of the awards went to acts that were once part of Stax Records in Memphis. Sam Moore and Dave Prater were known for intense harmonies, emotional delivery, and dancing. Booker T. Jones and the Memphis Group were originally the house band that set a standard for rhythm sections.

Other heroes of the rock'n'roll movement have been identified for collectors. *The Top 100 Rock'n'Roll Albums of All Time*[4] ranks albums by the tastes of music critics from seven countries. In both editions, 1977 and 1987, "Sgt. Pepper's Lonely Hearts Club Band" by the Beatles won first place. "Blonde on Blonde" by Bob

---

[4] Paul Gambaccini, *The Top 100 Rock'n'Roll Albums of All Time* (New York: Harmony Books, 1987).

Dylan ranked in the top three in both decades. The top-selling record of all time, forty million copies of "Thriller" by Michael Jackson, came in at number twenty-three. The list is interesting because albums respected as art are not always best sellers in the record stores, and vice versa. Fifty years may elapse before a change by some unknown musician is recognized as important and worthy of honor.

The horizon glitters with possibilities for young people starting out in the music business. Young hopefuls may imagine themselves international superstars. A few may see themselves as regional stars. Some hope for a place in the Hall of Fame. Others would be happy with a steady job playing their instrument, whereas still others never plan or hope beyond today. No single goal is everything for everyone. All set their sights according to their personal sense of ambition.

How to get from beginner to respected and successful musician is uppermost in the minds of those with high ambitions. Musicians who want to advance in rock'n'roll will find that the way up is in either concerts, recording, or songwriting.

If instrumentalists are happy playing before audiences, enjoy travel, and are not bothered by irregular hours, concerts may be a good choice. The road to advancement may lie in joining a better-known band. If they continue to practice or do gigs with bands, they will be in the music marketplace. That simply means they will be in touch with other musicians, who will refer them to other openings. As in all employment, people drop out for a variety of reasons, creating openings for others. Sickness, death, burnout, and bald heads are just a few. Young artists of rock music attract young buyers, who tend to pass over those bands with aging musicians. The exceptions are a few superstars who hang onto their fans, who are also growing bald. They grow old together.

The musician should think twice before moving to another band. A change might not be wise if much time has been invested in the current band. If fellow members seem to share the same ambitions, and more bookings are beginning to develop, a move may be a setback. The new offer may not be the advancement it appears to be at first. An example is a band that performed regularly and had 3,000 fans on their mailing list. A key player was lured away by an offer that failed to do what it promised, so he gained nothing and lost his former position. A band is a team that depends on all its members. To find another player is like starting from scratch, because the music style changes. Breaking from a group that has worked together for a long time is like breaking up a family, so don't change too quickly.

Another way for the musician to advance is to promote his or her current band. Of course, all band members need to be happy with the business order of the band and the musicianship. No salesman can sell a product he doesn't like. The object of promotion is to attract larger audiences, which in turn attract owners of larger clubs. In large music centers, a club operator will not hire a band for more than one night per month. They say that much time must elapse before all the band's fans will turn out for another evening. In the beginning, the band is booked for weekdays, then works up to Friday or Saturday. A band receives more money for working weekends. Since competition is not as fierce in smaller cities, it is possible to be booked for longer periods, thus increasing income. The key to this kind of advancement is popularity with audiences.

A few musicians have talent in songwriting, planning, managing, selling, and bookkeeping. They may put these talents to work by creating their own band and keeping these duties for themselves. Some band leaders team with their spouse to manage, promote, and keep financial records. The extra duties enable the multi-talented to collect a larger share of the band's income. Advancement is through increased income and the status of being a band leader.

If a musician invents tunes, feels the urge to set words to music, and knows how to write them down, perhaps songwriting would be a good choice. The road to advancement lies in finding a publisher, just as a band depends on finding a recording company. First the composer enrolls a copyright claim for the new work with the Library of Congress. The song is recorded on a demonstration tape, perhaps with other original songs. Only a voice and accompaniment are absolutely necessary, but rock music really needs drums, guitar, and keyboard to complete the effect.

Along with the demo, a typed lyric sheet is sent to the publisher. Also include a stamped self-addressed envelope if the tape is to be returned. If the publishers like the music, they will offer a contract giving the songwriter 50 percent of all royalties in return for their services. Publishers promote the song by publishing sheet music and using their contacts to find a cover artist. They find a recording company and arrange for mechanical licensing. All the precautions discussed in Chapter 3 on approaching record companies, dealing with sharks, and understanding contracts apply here as well. If the songwriter masters these hurdles, and the song is a hit, it will bring lifelong income. Several hit songs could give the songwriter ample retirement income.

If musicians are excited about their band and are good at drawing fans, perhaps recording is the way to advance and increase income. It is not an easy route, though it continues to draw aspiring young musicians like a magnet. Chapter 3 details many of the problems younger musicians face trying to break into recording.

The instrumentalist runs the risk of being bumped for studio musicians. Contracts can be misleading. Non-officials misrepresent themselves as recording tycoons. Promising bands break up over the confusion. Both songwriting and recording are big gambles, but like everything else in life, the greater the risk, the greater the gain.

Perhaps the logic of rock music's appeal is the way it absorbs the mind, emotions, and behavior of the listener. A person can be carried into another world, forgetting immediate cares. Rock is too lively to be background music. It calls for finger-tapping, shoulder movement, and dancing. Everybody needs to draw apart like this at times in their lives, but a few become spellbound. After a while the rock musician begins to mistake activity for progress. Exhilarating feelings today are not enough to support musicians tomorrow. Every musician needs to think about future advancement in his or her career.

WOMEN AND MINORITIES

"When I first began jamming with bands in high school, all the musicians were boys. Our attitudes were similar to the football team and the wrestling team. We were proving our macho-manhood, and girls just didn't belong. We didn't even have a female singer, although the rock band we saw on TV did. Grace Slick of the Jefferson Airplane was popular then and is still well known today. The servicemen returning from World War II brought back male comradeship that clung to our social habits for several decades. As boys, we found an outlet for male togetherness in rock music. The extra heavy beat seemed to speak the right amount of power, so we assumed girls would do little to further that effect." These reflections express the early attitudes of a rock musician toward women in rock'n'roll.

During the sixties, formerly all-male rock bands began to include women. Today most groups, like the Commitments, feature both men and women (AP/Wide World Photo).

Women in the twentieth century have been on an equal basis with men in popular music as composers, vocalists, and instrumentalists. Band leading, however, has been reserved for men. During World War II, while young men were in the service, Phil Spitalny and His All-Girl Orchestra were well known. The male emphasis in rock music began to break in the mid-sixties with women singers like Janis Joplin and mixed-gender groups like The Mamas and Papas. Opportunities for women in rock have made the biggest strides in the last ten to fifteen years. Women gathered into new wave bands known as The Bangles, The Go-Go's, and Tom

105

Tom Club. There also was a hard rock band called Girl's School.

With the advent of video, women have found a secure place in the rock music world. Video requires that performers be attractive and active. So while the musicians sit in one place with their instruments, rock singers have had to become rock dancers to survive. When video was new and unexplored, producers were not sure what to do with it. They asked Paula Abdul, the choreographer for the Los Angeles Lakers cheer team, to work up dances for singers Janet Jackson and Tracey Ullman. The idea of big dance shows along with rock music was a success. Later, Abdul learned to sing, and she is now featured as a rock singer/dancer on videos. Another female superstar is Madonna.

Bands with women musicians do have some managing problems. A woman needs a separate room on tour, whereas the men all pile into one room. If the band is mostly male, boyfriends or husbands can become jealous. Because of these issues, a new band may hesitate to include a woman. She may improve her chances by bringing these matters up for open discussion at the audition.

The business of rock music was slow to accept women, but it welcomed African Americans from the outset. The roots of rock are found in black culture. It was known about 1950 as rhythm and blues, one of many music styles from African Americans. Teenagers loved rhythm and blues, prompting radio stations to give more airtime to black artists such as Chuck Berry and Fats Domino. Soon after, Elvis Presley recorded a white version of the same rhythms, and it was renamed rock'n'roll. American businessmen saw an opportunity. They built a booming new industry that today honors artists of every race and nationality.

Both black and white artists held the attention of

white teens during the fifties. In its own way, rock'n'roll helped start the integration process, for this generation admired black musicians along with their own. They demanded rock'n'roll, without regard to color, on radio, in recordings, and in concerts. But their parents were suspicious. Teenagers would conform to their parents' and teachers' wishes by dressing up and dancing to Big Band music at high school proms. Before the evening was over, however, the girls would kick off their high heels and the boys would persuade the band to play rock'n'roll. It was not until a black man named Chubby Checker recorded The Twist in the sixties that rock became acceptable to everyone. The Twist was a nice little dance that everyone could do, so rock lost its subculture image. Before that turning point, Elvis Presley had been suspected by older adults of being a maniac out to ruin society. When he joined the army, his image changed, helping to bring rock'n'roll into the mainstream. Appreciation of black music and black musicians spread across all age groups.

Black Urban or "rap" is at the top of the music sales charts today. Blacks around New York retained disco rhythm but added their own lyrics. By talking to the time of the beat, rather than singing, Grand Master Flash pioneered rap but never received credit for it. Meanwhile, inner-city blacks taught their children in rap's unique style and language. Then in the late eighties record companies brought rap to the general public through the artistry of M.C. Hammer and C.C. Music Factory. Troupes of street dancers fill rap videos.

The future for minorities in rock music is optimistic. The business of rock began with acceptance of black talent, and ever since skin color has not been a drawback. Rock has been enriched by exotic effects and instruments from cultures around the world. "Sgt.

107

Pepper's Lonely Hearts Club Band" by the Beatles bore the mark of East Indian music as early as 1967.

Discrimination is not the main problem for minorities in rock. The problem is that they have not gained financially commensurate with their gifts to music and the whole entertainment field. Their songs have been copied, and they have been cheated out of income from performances and recordings. The world has been gladdened by music that began with African Americans almost forty years ago, and they are still struggling to be paid for it. This deficiency can be traced directly to the business side of music and the failure of young artists to protect themselves from unscrupulous operators. It is a problem for all musicians, but it is greater for blacks because they have given so much.

This book is intended to be a guide through the business of rock for all musicians, including minorities, blacks, and women. The inequities that have been part of rock can be changed by musicians who learn about the business before they begin.

RELATED POSITIONS

For various reasons, musicians retire from playing instruments and find happiness doing other work that is closely associated with rock music. It is possible to stay close to the rock business without being on stage, or writing songs, or recording. Some of these occupations were discussed in earlier chapters as related to the band. Let us now examine them as possible careers for those who know rock music but feel their strengths lie elsewhere.

Band Manager

The work of band managers was described in Chapter 1 as doing extra duties for the welfare of the whole band. They arrange for places to practice, transportation, hotels while on tour, transfer of luggage and instruments. They call the doctor, help band members get along, and find ways to inspire positive morale. They collect income and pay it out according to the band's agreement. They keep business records if the band does not have a bookkeeper. Band managers organize the details for moving groups of people day after day. They must be skilled in the art of persuasion. They build their careers on experience working with beginning bands. They can learn more about management through college courses in business management.

Agent

The work of music agents was described in Chapter 1 as booking venues for the band to perform. Agents usually keep contact with several places of entertainment that depend on them for suitable acts. They judge a band by whether its style and experience make a good match with their venues. They sign contracts with bands for specified periods of time. They suggest changes to make the band more popular. Music agents are people who enjoy being with and talking to other people. They have the ability both to sense audience needs and to settle differences. Agents often learn sales and mediation in another field, such as real estate. They add to those skills knowledge of the many varieties of rock and awareness of current trends in popular music. They may further their business skills with college courses in marketing.

Recording Engineer

The work of recording engineers was described in Chapter 3 as operating the equipment that produces a master tape. They adjust the console, microphones, and instruments to make clear sounds. Engineers must have good hearing and mechanical aptitude. They need

109

knowledge of acoustics and training to use the equipment. Both can be learned in colleges that offer courses in music technology. Engineers may own their own studio or they may be associated with a recording company. They often join forces with producers who like their particular style of engineering.

Artist and Repertoire

The work of A&R persons was described in Chapter 3 as finding talent for recording. They narrow down the selection of bands for their company to record. They speak for the company in meetings with the band, and they plan promotional programs for the band. A&Rs must be data-oriented people who enjoy studying sales charts, demographics, and current events. They draw ideas from the data to forecast music trends. They must maintain contacts in the music scene. From this foundation, they derive a music profile for judging bands. The training program for an A&R is apprenticeship and general music industry courses in college.

Producer

The work of record producers was compared in Chapter 3 to product manufacturing. They must have on-the-job training in the music business and know each step of the process from writing songs to pressing plastic. They have a way of putting it all together in a musical style that sells. They build their reputation by their wide scope of experience. Investors will not back relative newcomers with money to produce new records with new bands. Producers must be risk-takers with strong will to overcome obstacles and assume command. They may contract their services to recording companies or they may work alone. They may benefit from all the college courses mentioned above plus a course for music consultants.

LEADS INTO OTHER FIELDS

If musicians wish to enter fields one step further away from rock, their chances for success can be improved. Every school has a counseling department where tests can be taken to determine a person's interests and aptitudes. Certain psychologists specialize in career testing. Musicians can learn much about their own abilities if they know what to look for and are willing to spend the time on self-analysis.

Jobs can be classified into three groups according to the worker's focus: on data, people, or things. The instrumentalist's focus is on things. A musical instrument is his or her primary interest. The focus on things may carry over to other activities, such as food if cooking is a hobby, or pencils if drawing is an attraction.

The musician may have a secondary focus on data or people. Examples of data focus are reading history or analyzing maps and graphs. Examples of people focus are helping others, selling, or teaching. The instrumentalist may be working with a thing, but the need for change may point to a different tendency. By analyzing one's own daily activities and feelings about them, one may gain a better understanding of self. These three areas of job focus—data, people, things—help to identify strengths and weaknesses related to occupation. They are worth looking into before making on uneducated move into another field.

The occupations listed below, besides those discussed above, fall into the three categories of data, people, or things. Experience or knowledge of the rock business is helpful background for each of them.

Additional training may be needed to qualify for some of this work. State universities, colleges, community colleges, and private schools across the nation provide courses in commercial music. Within the last five years, New York University offered courses in Music Business and Technology; Madonna College in Michigan offered courses in Music Management; Florida State University offered courses in Music Research; and Harold Luick and Associates, a private school in Carlisle, Iowa, offered courses for Music Industry Consultants. College offerings change from year to year, so the career-changer is advised to check current catalogs.

High schools and public libraries in some communities have school catalogs available for student use. *Handel's National Directory for the Performing Arts, Vol. 2, Educational Institutions*[5] supplies addresses to write for catalogues. The book lists courses for all the arts, but music listings are easily identified. The schools are grouped by state, and each listing includes information on student loans and types of degrees offered.

THING ORIENTATION

Place of Entertainment
Stage Acoustician—Responsible for the quality of the stage, theater, or auditorium to aid hearing or transmit sound. Building surfaces, furniture, and speakers can be adjusted to enhance the band's music and improve hearing in every direction. Good hearing and knowledge of acoustics needed.

Sound Equipment Operator—Responsible for operation of the sound board, microphones, and speakers during programs. Assures best-quality sound and corrects noise and distortion. Good hearing and experience with equipment needed.

---

[5] *Handel's National Directory for the Performing Arts, Vol. 2, Educational Institutions*, Beatrice Handel, founding editor (Dallas: NOPA, Inc., 1988).

Recording Company

Vault Manager—Responsible for keeping company-owned master tapes safe from damage, copying, and theft. Keeps written records on location of tapes and who checks them out. Release date of a recording determines whether it can be checked out. Alertness and knowledge of security principles needed.

Advertising Artist—Responsible for design and finished art of record covers, posters, handouts. Works on a deadline according to release date of a record. Artistic ability, skills in art media, and knowledge of printing processes needed.

Record Manufacturer—Responsible for pressing plastic to reproduce the master tape. Operates machine or owns business that provides this service. Experience with equipment needed.

Technology

Instrument Builder—Responsible for construction of guitars, drums, keyboards, etc. Handmade instruments are highly valued for their unique sound. Good hand-eye coordination and knowledge of instrument building needed.

Instrument Repair—Responsible for supply of parts, attachment of parts, and mending, splicing, and tuning of instruments. Good hand-eye coordination and knowledge of instrument repair needed.

Piano and Organ Tuner—Responsible for adjusting sound to musical scale or pitch of orchestra. Good hearing and knowledge of instrument tuning needed.

Road Crew—Responsible for transport, set-up, and connection of instruments, sound equipment, and stage props for an act on tour. Does simple repair and tuning of instruments. Physical strength and general knowledge of several instruments needed.

DATA ORIENTATION

Publishing Company

Music Editor—Responsible for preparing a songwriter's works for publication by selection, arrangement, and explanatory notes. Ability to read music and knowledge of printing and publishing needed.

Music Grapher—Responsible for layout and drawing of music score on page in preparation for printer. Ability to read music, drawing skills, and knowledge of printing needed.

Proofreader—Responsible for reading printer's proofs of sheet music to find errors and make corrections before final print. Ability to read music and attention to detail needed.

Entertainment Business

Music Attorney—Advises musicians and others in the music industry in matters of the law. Represents them in negotiations and lawsuits. May legally act for a client. Knowledge of the music industry, degree in law, and a specialty in entertainment and the arts needed.

Music Accountant—Designs system for recording financial exchanges. Keeps, inspects, and makes reports for the music industry. Knowledge of the music industry, degree in accounting, and CPA designation needed.

Bookkeeper—Responsible for calculating royalties and mechanical fees due the songwriter, publisher, and recording artist. Mathematical ability and knowledge of music contracts and mechanical rights law needed.

Literature

Music Historian—Inquires, analyzes, coordinates, and explains musical events of the past. Writes books, lectures, and teaches courses on the subject. Curiosity about music and writing, speaking, or teaching skill needed.

Discographer—Studies and catalogs phonograph records according to performer, musical style, or sales. Collects information from which music charts are made. Research, graphing, and writing skills needed.

Music Critic—Responsible for writing articles on music for newspapers or journals. Analyzes, compares, contrasts, interprets, and judges music. Discernment about music and writing skills needed.

Music Librarian—Responsible for collection, arrangement, and care of music books, pamphlets, sheet music, and recordings. Keeps records on circulation. Knowledge of music and degree in library science needed.

PEOPLE ORIENTATION

Music Entertainment Business

Club/Theater Operator—Owns or manages business location providing entertainment for the public. Oversees service people and supplies for restaurant, bar, and stage. Advertises for patrons. People skills and knowledge and experience in business management needed.

Concert Organizer—Coordinates music events for the public. Arranges for location, contracts for artists, meets city and state requirements, oversees advertising and ticket sales. People skills, money, and experience in meetings and conventions needed.

Broadcast Announcer—Responsible for introducing acts or recordings to the audience through radio. Ability to divert people, impromptu speaking skill, and knowledge of radio broadcasting needed.

Recording or Publishing Company

Publisher—Finds original songs with popular appeal,

115

contracts with songwriter, arranges for sheet music, recording, and mechanical licenses. Ability to mediate differences and knowledge of trends in music, copyright law, and music contracts needed.

Promotion—Responsible for procuring concerts and planning itinerary of tour. Tours with band and arranges for radio, TV, and record store appearances. Sales ability and general knowledge of music and broadcast industries needed.

Marketing—Responsible for planning and overseeing production of all advertising graphics. Schedules advertising by release date of record. Sales ability and experience in advertising art needed.

Public Relations—Responsible for procuring newspaper ads and articles. Advises band on how to handle media interviews. Writes articles about band for publication. Sales ability and writing skill needed.

Sales—Responsible for selling and supplying records to retail outlets and radio stations. Sales ability and knowledge of record industry needed.

Technology
Rental and Sales Outlet—Owns or manages business that rents or sells musical instruments. Oversees sales clerks and inventory. People skills and knowledge of business management needed.

Education
Music Teacher—Imparts basic knowledge about instrument and music system to children and adults. Educates their latent abilities to express music. Skill on instrument and knowledge of teaching methods needed.

Music Museum—Owner or director responsible for the collection, arrangement, and care of music memorabilia for viewing by the public. Knowledge of music and teaching skills and design skills needed.

Our imaginary band that formed in high school, gained fans, and worked their way up to concerts and a recording will progress more slowly in the nineties. The demand for musicians was expected to grow, but the recession has changed that prediction for the present. Band members might find music jobs in other fields, such as advertising, until prospects improve as expected before the year 2000.

As for advancement in music, the avenues up are through changing to a better-known band or improving the present one, songwriting, and recording. But when the whole industry is down, moving up is difficult. It is the economy, not being female or ethnic, that holds musicians back. Women and blacks have been welcome and encouraged in rock music since the mid-'60s.

Work experience is never wasted, but serves as a building block for the next endeavor. The rock music business is practical education for several other occupations, although more specialized training may be required.

Now, the big question—could you make a living in rock music? We've had this industry under the magnifying glass to learn everything we could about it. It's time to learn more about your attitudes, talents, and preferences to see if you'd be a good match for this business.

6

Evaluating a Career in Rock

"Am I the kind of person who would do well in rock music? I seem to have a natural talent on my instrument. I enjoy working with the band, and I follow through with them. I am known as a musician among my classmates. They like our music and ask us to play for parties." A young adult asks this question, and the answer is that he has a good beginning.

The basic elements for success in rock music were mentioned—instrumental skills, musical and social cooperation with the band, listening audiences. This person would do well with music as a leisure activity. He might volunteer his services for community dances or provide entertainment for fundraising events. He might also enter songwriting competitions and win prizes. Others would admire his talent and generosity. He would have a recognized position among the people who know him. But he would not fit into the business of rock music without several other frames of mind.

The serious student of careers does more than investigate rock music. Knowledge of self—attitudes, talents, satisfactions, opinions—help a person find out if he is the key that fits the lock, the piece that completes the puzzle. A description of the person who would do well in rock gives a picture of what is needed. The student may find out if he fits the picture in a variety of ways. Converse with friends, for friends usually see our talents and interests better than we do. Talk to a career counselor who can administer personality and aptitude tests. Zero in on your own feelings and attitudes, making notes of what you enjoy, tolerate, or detest. Those most successful in finding the career that meets their needs and desires are those who understand themselves in depth.

No problem can be solved without first finding out the facts. The facts have been covered on what the rock music business is really like. Now we shall describe the attitudes and talents of the musician so that students may compare them with their own attitudes and talents.

FAVORABLE ATTITUDES

Competition consists of several people competing for one prize. The mind of the rock musician should thrive on competition, because there are so many young people competing for so few prizes. Each step of the way from band affiliation, audience support, good bookings, and recording contracts to media appearances is a continual race. Musicians run as if they were in a race, with one eye on the goal and the other on the runner who is gaining on them.

Their performance has to be better than that of other instrumentalists, not just adequate. They have to find a band and songwriter with popular appeal, then constantly compare with what other bands are doing to win audiences. The band has to win the favor of entertainment businessmen over other competitors who want the same job. Winning the favor of a recording company is more of a mystery, because the competition is unknown. They still compete, however, by making the demo as close to perfection as possible and making the A&R person's job easier in all other respects. Musicians keep in mind the idea of competing for so few prizes in everything they do. It becomes a way of life.

Only a few win the popular acclaim that follows

media exposure. National television audiences respond to what is familiar. Those who finally appear on MTV receive national recognition and thus become superstars. Since room at the top is limited, the majority of musicians never break through to superstar status. Therefore, would-be musicians must decide whether they are willing to settle for less. Would they be happy competing for every booking knowing that that is as far as they will go? Do they enjoy the act of competing whether or not it takes them to the top of the rock music ladder? You might compare this attitude with that of the professional football player. Only a few ever go to the Superbowl, but the excitement of competing in each game is enough to keep him challenged with football.

Because competitive musicians constantly keep their eye on the goal, they never stop seeking ways to get there. They are determined to find a better route, to try different methods, to experiment with new ideas. They are not the kind of people who find a job, then are content to stay in it for the rest of their life. If the object is fans and more fans, they think outside the bounds of usual behavior to find them.

In recent years, several bands have begun playing benefits or producing records on behalf of the homeless or some other cause. Willie Nelson and his group have done Farm Aid concerts every year for five years. A good side effect has been to expand Nelson's audiences at the same time. Segments of the public who would not go to a concert for their own enjoyment did buy tickets to benefit others. Creative thinking is essential for the musician who would compete in the music marketplace. The creativity associated with music has to expand to creativity in business, too.

A career in rock music requires dedication that is single-minded and doesn't look back at what could have been. Unfortunately, dedication to music is often confused with being hypnotized by music. Teenagers have many interests from which to draw career ideas. The problem with music is its magnetism, the party atmosphere, and the admiring crowds. This occurs in high school at a time in life when social needs take first place. Young musicians then make decisions about their life's work based on a few school experiences. They give more time to rehearsals and gigs, while other interests fade.

While still in school, a singer said, "Music is the only thing I know how to do." Upon graduation she went to Hollywood with thousands of other young people with stars in their eyes. As the years went by, her optimism faded under the pressure of competition, shady business ethics, and other vices that thrive on naiveté. Even for a competitive person, the music business is inordinately tough. Videos and television place a few stars within reach of millions, depriving many other talented musicians of work. The singer, who felt she could not do anything else, then had to face the passing years with worry.

Young adults need to be aware of all the facts before making a premature decision to enter this career. They need especially to be wary of cutting off other interests by specializing too soon. They should choose music only if they could not be fulfilled in any other career. The determination to succeed in rock music should be built on the foundation of careful exploration and comparison of several career possibilities.

Besides competitive spirit, creative thinking, and dedication, one other habitual attitude enables the musician to prosper. That is the ability to discern the unspoken goals, working patterns, and ethics of others. A musician must either be very people-oriented or have a close alliance with someone who is. Many excellent

121

musicians, with superb skill and great imagination on their instruments, have not been able to advance in the music business. All their discernment went into the tools of the business, not into the people they had to work with.

Making a living as a musician requires the element of people perception. A player may make beautiful music with members of the band, but those members must be people with similar long-range purposes. A guitarist who played in a rock group also played in a mariachi band. The mariachi band received more bookings during the holidays, so the rock group was stranded without him on guitar. His ambition and disregard of others showed up in missed rehearsals long before the missed bookings. A people-understanding musician is more likely to see the problem coming and take steps to prevent trouble before it is too late.

A likeable songwriter-guitarist in another band took on the extra job of finding places for live performances. His style of rock was fast and loud, but the clubs he approached catered to more subdued dinner and dancing patrons. He was so absorbed in his own form of expression that he thought everyone liked what he liked. A people-oriented musician would have steered this songwriter in another direction, seeing that his working style did not suggest sales ability.

A keyboardist with many years of experience both in concerts and recording joined another existing band. She memorized the new songs, spent hours at rehearsals, and was prompt and cooperative at performances. Occasionally a check from a club operator bounces and the musicians are not paid until the manager can collect; sometimes the payment is never collected. This time the keyboardist learned that everybody had been paid but her. Remembering other instances when she had not been paid, she learned the hard way that others were not as ethical as she. Not every coworker will be a saint, but precautionary bookkeeping practices, direct communication, and courts of justice can help to raise low ethical standards. Setbacks such as these should be dealt with before they become big problems. It takes musicians who study their coworkers with the same care they give their music.

The young adult who asked whether he would do well in rock might rephrase his question. He could ask, "How do I compare with others in competitive spirit, creative thinking, determination, and people perception?" Then he could run a poll among friends and teachers. The results might give a clearer picture of how he ranks in those essential attitudes for a career in the rock music business.

HELPFUL TALENTS

Audiences know that every band rehearses before walking on stage. Other necessary actions, not so obvious to fans, help to bridge the gap between the first gathering of the group and bookings. If the band is organized as a proprietorship, musicians are employed solely for their musical abilities. The usual plan is a partnership in which musical abilities and other talents are pooled. Because beginning bands cannot afford to hire others to do these extra tasks, the band members divide the work among themselves. Applicants for positions in a band improve their chances if they know what their talents are and spell out at the audition how they can help.

Managerial actions have to do with the welfare of the entire band. Finding places to rehearse, making travel arrangements, reserving hotel space while on tour, transferring luggage and instruments, and collecting income and paying it out are examples of tasks that a manager would do if the band could afford outside help. Until that time, someone in the band volunteers.

123

Band members pool talents in management, sales, and book-keeping in addition to rehearsing music, before walking on stage. The resulting performance, like this of Living Color's, can be spectacular (AP/Wide World Photo).

Sales actions have to do with promoting the band's reputation to expand audience following. These tasks include producing advertisements and a press kit, networking with professionals, finding places to perform, and acting as Master of Ceremonies. A music agent finds bookings for the band, and advertising agencies do the ads for a commission. Two sales jobs, however, can never be farmed out. Someone in the band is always responsible for networking and building charisma with the audiences in the role of M.C.

Bookkeeping actions have to do with keeping accurate financial records of income, expenses, and payroll. The person who volunteers for these duties does not collect money, pay it out, or sign checks. He does balance bank statements, keep a journal of money exchanges, file tax reports, and make regular bookkeeping reports to all band members.

If the student thinking about a career in rock music passed the attitude poll, he might explore his talents further. The counseling department in public schools usually will arrange aptitude tests for students. However, talents are only prospects until the student takes action to develop them through courses, reading, and volunteer work. In time, he may develop definite skills in managing, selling, or bookkeeping that, along with musical ability, will make him a sought-after band member.

SATISFACTIONS

The dictionary definition of music—the art and science of the formal organization of tone—does not begin to explain its enormous attraction. Music appears to have been a part of societies living before the Greeks and Romans. The Book of Psalms contains the lyrics of songs passed from parents to children long before they were written down three thousand years ago. Every human emotion from praise and joy to anger and despair was expressed through these songs. Something in the heart of humans needs the emotional outlet of sound and tone.

Perhaps a clue to the appeal of music among instrumentalists lies in a scientific study of workers' brains. Through magnetic resonance imaging, it was found that musicians use more of the brain at once than any other worker. It is speculated that this may account for the feeling of being more alive reported by musicians. "Creating spontaneously, in harmony with other people, uniting synergetically with other musicians is very

125

exciting," according to an early rock'n'roll artist who later moved into jazz.

Some people are drawn to music more than others. They are the ones who want to do more than listen to it. They want to write songs, play the instruments, work in a band, and see others enjoy it all. The satisfactions of being a rock musician are best expressed by the musicians themselves, so we asked the question, "What is it about playing in a rock band that satisfies you?"

An Indian entertainer from a New Mexico reservation answered, ". . . the fun of working with a team. Getting our act together . . . the unity of spirit."

A religious rock composer/singer with a music ministry said, "I have a message. This is the best way for a woman to deliver that message to the most people. I can't write: I'm not a public speaker: I do have songs in my head."

". . . entertaining others, making them happy in what sometimes seems like a bleak world. It's great to see the smiles and know we contributed something," reported a drummer from a black band. A forerunner of rock was the New Orleans marching band, which marched to funerals playing slow laments but returned playing quadrilles in quick-step time. Funerals became celebrations with the help of happy music like "Tiger Rag" and "Maple Leaf Rag" played by these early bands.

"I stay in music because people treat me with respect," explained a young man who takes pride in developing his craft.

The satisfactions of a career in rock music depend on the person who is reporting. Perhaps from these quotations the questioning student may find an explanation of why he or she is drawn to this career. Is it the need to tell the world something important? Is it the need to become the best on an instrument? Is it the pleasure of working with others for a common purpose? Is it the love of making others happy? Young adults looking into this career also look into themselves to understand the attraction. To tolerate the demands music will put on them, they must be thoroughly committed to its importance for self-fulfillment.

CHECKLIST

So far the career searching student has explored the facts about rock music and more facts about self. Now it is time to answer thoughtfully each of these questions to determine true feelings about specific problems. What a pity for a person to put in all the effort it takes to be a band member and then find that he or she is intimidated by aggressive people. The business end of music is full of assertive individuals. Musicians meet and work with many people, but if privacy is important they could become annoyed with so much people contact. A music career colors every facet of life from sleeping hours to residence to public appearance to cultivation of friends. A careful evaluation of each point listed will help uncover those areas that might later present problems. A problem for one person may not be a problem for another. If nothing else, an analysis of the answers should reveal the weak points a student might work to fortify.

Are my instrumental skills up to professional standard?
Am I creative with music?
Do I bounce back from rejection?
Am I afraid to ask business questions?
Am I afraid to press for fairness?
Do I understand business proprietorships and partnerships?
Can I handle my own taxes, insurance, retirement fund?

127

Am I a team worker?

Do I have another talent to help the band?

Do I understand the recording process?

Am I intimidated by aggressive people?

Am I a self-starter?

Can I adapt to late hours, travel, weekend and holiday work?

Can I manage my expenses on an irregular income?

Am I willing to move to another location?

Can I live with the constraints of close relationships?

Can I resist drugs, junk food, the sedentary life?

Do I have stage presence?

Am I prepared to compete for every booking?

Do the satisfactions of music outweigh the disadvantages?

Teenagers are often asked by their parents, teachers, and classmates what they plan to do with their lives. The day I told my mother I wanted to be a musician was the day her hair started to turn gray. She visualized me living in a smoke- and drug-filled environment. She concluded that I would not settle down with a family and give her grandchildren. She imagined me destitute in old age and other depressing stereotypes. It was a point of contention between us because we both possessed vague notions about the life of a rock musician.

Facts about this business can help students and other interested persons out of the fog of misunderstanding. It can help them think clearly about the effects of a career in rock music on the whole spectrum of life. If the student has studied all aspects of the business and self and appears to be a good match, this is the career to pursue. Rock music does not have the upstanding reputation of medicine or law, because it is so public. If a rock star makes a mistake, the newspapers advertise it to the world. After a few incidents, all rock musicians are thrown into the "bad apple" category. Some rock stars have died of drug overdose, but so have doctors, and both are exposed to the temptation on a daily basis. Musicians move often, have unsteady incomes, and compete for every job. The same can be said of salesmen, but no mother complains about her child becoming a salesman.

This book began with a story about a drummer who pursued rock music despite early resistance from his parents, who couldn't imagine why he was so attracted to the drums. None of the relatives were musicians. He had not been encouraged in that direction by anyone. He just seemed to have an inner drive that needed to be expressed. Years later, it was learned that his great grandfather was a drummer in the Civil War. This man was so attached to his drum that he was still playing it the day he died, sixty years later, at age ninety-five. The urge to musical expression is stronger in some people than in others. The challenge to parents is to accept that difference and honor it.

Glossary

A&R Artist and Repertoire, the person or department of the record company that selects and signs artists and oversees them in the company relationship.

advance Money paid to the songwriter or recording artist before regular royalty payments begin. Advances are deducted from royalties. Also called "upfront" money.

AFM (American Federation of Musicians) A union for musicians and arrangers.

AIMP Association of Independent Music Publishers.

airplay The radio broadcast of a recording.

arrangement Adaptation of a musical composition for performance or recording.

ASCAP (American Society of Composers, Authors, and Publishers), a performing rights organization.

A side Side one of a single, promoted by the record company to become a hit.

assign To transfer a right to another, usually from writer to publisher.

BMA Black Music Association.

BMI (Broadcast Music, Inc.), a performing rights organization.

B side Side two of a single.

board The console of controls designed for recording and mixing.

booking Engagement secured for musicians to perform in a place of entertainment and to be paid for their services.

booking agent Person who solicits work and schedules performances for musicians.

catalog   A band's history of records made with one record company or publisher and controlled by them.

CD   *See* compact disc.

charts   Top 100 Albums collected by *Billboard*, Top Concert Grosses collected by *Amusement Business*, and other sales results by the weekly trade magazines.

compact disc   Small disc, about 4.5 inches in diameter, that is read by a laser beam in a CD player. On the disc, digitized music is stored as microscopic pits in an aluminum base.

controlled   composition   Song   with   copyright, publisher right, and mechanical license already established.

copyright   Songwriter's exclusive right to the publication, production, performance, or sale of rights of a song.

cover   An artist's recording of a songwriter's song.

cover version   Rerecording of a song previously released by another artist.

crossover   A record that crosses over from one music style to another; a rock/country crossover is one that originates in rock and crosses over to country.

cut   Any finished recording, a selection from an LP, or to record.

demo   Demonstration on tape, made for purpose of interesting record companies in the band.

disc   A piece of recording vinyl.

distributor   Person or company that markets records and keeps retailers in stock, being licensed to do so in a particular location.

doublefold   Package designed to hold discs.

dubs   Copies made from master tape recording.

EP   A record with cumulative playing time of less than thirty-five minutes.

engineer   Technician who runs the recording board, translating the music through the equipment.

evergreen Any song that remains popular year after year.

exploit To seek legal use of a song for income.

gig Performance by a band before an audience.

Gold Award for 500,000 copies sold of an album, 1,000,000 copies of a single.

Harry Fox Agency Organization that collects mechanical royalties.

hit Song that makes the Top 100 in sales and airplay.

hook Memorable phrase or melody that catches attention and is repeated often in a song.

IMU International Music Union.

instrumentalist Person who performs on a musical instrument.

IPS (inches per second), a speed designation for tape recording.

jamming Improvising by several musicians.

LP A record with a cumulative playing time of thirty-five or more minutes.

label Name of record company or brand name of record it produces.

logo Promotional artwork of a particular design to remind the public of a specific recording artist or company.

lyric sheet Typed or written copy of a song's lyrics.

market Potential song or music buyers; demographic area of the record-buying public.

master The final edited and mixed, highest-quality tape recording, from which copies will be made.

mechanical license Right to reproduce records and broadcast them, usually according to a fee arrangement.

mix To blend a multitrack recording into the desired balance of sound.

monaural Single source of sound, such as standard one-track tape.

MOR Middle of the road, easy listening.

multitrack recording Recording four or more audio signals on magnetic tape, then mixing them down to two-track stereo mix.

music publisher Company that evaluates songs for commercial possibilities, finds artists to record them, finds other uses such as TV or film, collects income, protects copyrights.

NAIRD National Association of Independent Record Distributors.

NARM National Association of Record Merchandisers.

NMPA National Music Publishers Association.

payola Dishonest payment to broadcaster for airplay.

piracy Unauthorized reproduction and sale of printed or recorded music.

Platinum Award for 1,000,000 copies sold of an album, 2,000,000 million copies sold of a single.

pop Popular songs of today, humorous, and youth-oriented.

plug Favorable mention of a song; to pitch a song.

producer Person who directs production of a record, overseeing song selections, arrangements, musicians, and engineer.

public domain Status of a song after the copyright term—the composer's life plus fifty years—has expired.

publish To reproduce music in a saleable form and distribute to the public by sale.

R&B Rhythm and blues, forerunner of rock'n'roll.

records Devices by which sound is preserved for later transmission to listeners, such as discs, tapes, cartridges.

recording artist Featured musician on a record, usually signed to a label.

release Any record issued by a record company.

repertoire The stock of songs a musician is ready to perform.

rhythm machine Electronic device that provides

133

various tempos for use as background rhythm for other instuments.

RIAA Recording Industry Association of America.

royalties Composers' income from use of their songs, and recording artists' income from sales of records.

press To manufacture a record.

self-contained Of a band or act that write all their own material.

showcase Presentation of new artists or songs.

sideman Musician who aids the performance of recording artists with instrumental skills.

single A song released off an album that is considered the most commercial for radio and sales; 45 rpm record with only one song per side. A 12-inch single refers to a long version of a song, usually used for dance music.

song shark Person who deals with songwriters deceptively for their own profit.

statutory royalty rate Minimum payment for mechanical rights guaranteed by law that a record company must pay the songwriter and his publisher for each record or tape sold.

stiff The first recording of a song that fails commercially.

subpublishing Certain rights granted by a U.S. publisher to a foreign publisher to promote the U.S. catalog in his territory.

sweeten To add parts to existing records to enhance the sound.

take Attempt to record, or an acceptable recording of performance.

trades Publications that cover the music industry.

venue The place where the action occurs; in England, club or theater where entertainment is presented.

vocalist Singer, may be associated with a band.

Appendix A
Bookkeeping

The band that is a business partnership should open a bank account in the name of the band. Any band members can make deposits to this account, but only one member can make withdrawals to pay expenses. The musician authorized to act as manager usually gives the bank his signature for signing checks. If all expenses are paid by check, the check register could serve as a record of money exchanges. A separate journal is needed to record expenses when paid by both check and cash.

The musician authorized to act as bookkeeper makes entries in this journal. Purchase ledger sheets from an office supply store or rule notebook paper into five columns as illustrated below. This simplified journal keeps a running total of the balance, or money remaining in the account, just like a check register.

When the manager writes a check to pay expenses, the bookkeeper records it in the Expense column. When cash is paid out to pay expenses by someone in the band, that also is recorded in the Expense column. It is advisable to announce that there will be no reimbursement without a receipt as evidence of purchase.

Start-up costs are often shared equally by band members before they play a gig and earn money. These investments by the band members are recorded in the Income column. It remains in the account for the duration of the band to cover unexpected costs. Whenever the balance goes below the amount invested, the band knows it is not making a profit. The balance will not go over this amount for very long, because income from gigs is paid out immediately. This money is also recorded under the Income column. When the band disbands and all the bills have been paid, the balance in the account is divided equally among the band members who made initial investments.

JOURNAL FOR VELVET TOOTHACHE

DATE	ENTRIES	EXPENSE	INCOME	BALANCE
7/10	Jose Rives, investment		100.00	
7/12	Betty Moss, investment		100.00	
7/12	Bob Smith, investment		100.00	
7/13	Andre Jones, investment		100.00	400.00
7/15	Rehearsal Hall, July rent	120.00		280.00
7/16	Office Supply, ledger sheets	10.00		270.00
7/30	Print Shop, fliers	40.00		230.00
8/10	Jimmy's, 3 hours		360.00	590.00
8/11	$590 - 400 \times 0.25 = 47.50$			
	Jose Rives, 25%	47.50		
	Betty Moss, 25%	47.50		
	Bob Smith, 25%	47.50		
	Andre Jones, 25%	47.50		400.00
8/15	Rehearsal Hall, August rent	120.00		280.00
8/23	Print Shop, fliers	20.00		260.00
9/3	Gasoline, Wilcox trip	20.00		240.00
9/3	Benson Hotel, lodging	60.00		180.00
9/3	Riverside Ballroom, 3 hours		500.00	680.00
9/4	$680 - 400 \times 0.25 = 70.00$			
	Jose Rives, 25%	70.00		
	Betty Moss, 25%	70.00		
	Bob Smith, 25%	70.00		
	Andre Jones, 25%	70.00		400.00

A line is drawn between each booking and the expenses that led up to it. This last part may be photo-copied and given to each band member with his pay. With statements, the band members keep informed about financial matters and are better prepared to make decisions as a group.

Appendix B
Recording Contract

A simplified version of a recording contract is given for teaching and study purposes. This model is not a substitute for a contract tailored by a music attorney for the specific needs of a company and a band. The names and addresses are fictitious and in no way represent any existing record company, rock band, or law offices.

PRETEND RECORDS
12345 Imagination Place
Record City, California, 90999 USA
20 July 1993

Ms Mary Bates (a/k/a Contrary Mary)
Mr Paul Katz
Mr Ernesto Rodriguez
Mr Lucius Johnson
Collectively known professionally as "Velvet Toothache"
54321 Make Believe Lane
Record City, California, 90909

Gentlemen and Ms Bates:
This agreement, when signed by you and by us, will mean you record for us and no other. This includes video and sound-only recordings.

1) TERM
A) You will record for us from 20 July 1993. The end will be one hundred twenty (120) days after the date of first United States commercial release of our first LP.

2) RECORDING PLEDGE

A) You have recorded the basic tracks for thirteen (13) master recordings (listed in Schedule A). The tapes for these masters will be delivered to our studio, where they will be made into finished products under our direction. More masters will be recorded only if we both agree.

3) OPTION

A) If we sell twenty thousand (20,000) records, we may extend the term of this agreement for one (1) year. The records are to be sold through United States record stores. The records will be the first LP produced under this agreement. They are to be sold within one hundred twenty (120) days of release. If the term is extended, we will record masters for a second LP.

B) If the term of this agreement is extended, we will notify you by registered mail.

C) If the term of this agreement is extended, we will pay you five thousand dollars ($5,000) as an advance on your royalties.

4) GRANT OF RIGHTS

A) You give to us the continuing, worldwide right to manufacture, advertise, distribute, license, and sell copies of the records made under this agreement.

5) PROMOTIONAL VIDEO CLIPS

A) Fifty percent (50%) of all money we advance to make promotional clips will be returned to us out of your royalties. Any income from the clips will be split equally by you and us.

B) You and we will supervise the making of these videos. You and we will approve the expenses of these videos in writing.

6) CO-OWNERSHIP OF MASTERS

A) All masters recorded under this agreement will be registered in your and our joint names. Fifty percent (50%) of the money we advance for registration will be returned to us out of your royalties. You give us the continuing, worldwide right to manufacture, distribute, and sell records made under this agreement. We may assign this right to others. We may use any trademark, trade name, or label. We may license others to sell. We may use your name and pictures with these rights.

7) RECORDING AND PACKAGING ELEMENTS

A) You have recorded the basic tracks for thirteen (13) masters (listed in Schedule A). The finishing will be done by Chuck Lester at a studio of our choice. The recording of other masters will be by our mutual consent. Accompaniment and songs will be chosen by mutual consent.

B) All packaging artwork and design will be selected by mutual consent. The cost to be paid by us will be in writing and approved by us before design begins.

8) RECOVERY OF RECORDING AND MISCELLANEOUS COSTS

A) All money we advance to pay for recording will be returned to us out of your royalties. The cost to be paid by us will be in writing and approved by us before recording begins.

B) The term "recording costs" means all costs in the making of masters. It does not include manufacturing or distribution costs. It does include a) all payments to musicians, vocalists, conductors, arrangers, orchestrators, contractors, and copyists. It includes union scale payments, payroll taxes, fees to the producer, rental and delivery of instruments. b) It includes travel, hotel, and living expenses of musicians, producers, and other personnel attending recording sessions. c) It includes studio, engineering, tape, editing, mastering, and other costs of making final master. d) It includes other expenses usually considered "recording costs."

C) All money paid by us for you shall be recovered from your royalties, unless we give written consent not to.

9) RECORDING ARTIST ROYALTIES

A) Your recording artist royalty is based on one hundred percent (100%) of net sales, less cost of manufacturing and containers. Each sale is to be at suggested retail list price (SRLP). Sales are to be through United States record stores.

B) Your base royalty rate on single and EP records is ten percent (10%) of the SRLP on net sales through United States record stores.

C) Your base royalty rate on LP records is twelve percent (12%) of the SRLP on net sales through United States record stores.

D) Your royalty rate on record club sales and budget line records is fifty percent (50%) of the base royalty rate. Record club sales and budget line records are priced between fifty percent (50%) and sixty-five percent (65%) of the regular SRLP.

E) Your royalty rate on sales to United States government, educational institutions, libraries, and mid-priced records is seventy-five percent (75%) of the base royalty rate. United States government includes its subdivisions, departments, agencies, and records sold for resale through military facilities. Mid-priced records are between sixty-six percent (66%) and eighty percent (80%) of the regular SRLP.

F) Your royalty rate on export sales is fifty percent (50%) of the base royalty rate.

G) You will receive fifty percent (50%) of income on:

a) foreign licenses; b) flat-fee licenses; and c) other licenses or sales.

H) Your royalties from foreign licensees will be figured in the currency we are paid. It will be figured at the same rate of exchange in which we are paid. Foreign and import taxes will be figured in the same way.

I) If any of your masters are put on a record with any other masters, your royalty share will be figured from the total number of royalty-bearing masters included.

J) No royalties will be paid on promotional copies, cutouts, distress sales, or sales at less than fifty percent (50%) of our wholesale price. Free goods will be limited to fifteen percent (15%) of LP records, and thirty percent (30%) of single and EP records shipped. These amounts are common in the industry.

K) Royalties will be withheld to pay for any advance payments to the musicians.

L) Before royalties are figured, manufacturing and container costs will be subtracted from SRLP. On LP records, or any item with LP-type packaging such as a twelve-inch single, twelve and one half percent (12 1/2%) will be subtracted. On doublefold or gatefold LP packaging, or a package with inserts, fifteen percent (15%) will be subtracted. On singles with picture bags, twelve and one half percent (12 1/2%) will be subtracted. On cassette tapes, twenty percent (20%) will be subtracted.

M) By net sales we mean gross sales less returns and credits.

10) MECHANICAL ROYALTIES

A) The Harry Fox license or similar license will apply. Maximum amount on singles will be two (2) times the smallest legal rate as of the single's first release in the United States. Maximum amount on EPs will be four (4) times the smallest legal rate as of the EP's first release in the United States. Maximum amount on LPs will be ten (10) times the smallest legal rate as of the LP's first release in the United States. If we arrange for distribution through a major label, the changes they require will apply to you.

B) If we do not pay artist royalties on records, we will not pay mechanical royalties either.

C) All songs recorded in masters under this agreement are licensed to us for the United States at the royalty rates set forth above. These songs may be written or composed by you, in whole or in part, alone or with others. These songs may be owned or controlled by you, in whole or in part. These songs may be owned or controlled by a person, firm, or corporation in which you have an interest.

D) No mechanical royalties will be paid on controlled compositions that are arrangements of songs in the public domain.

E) Copyright assignments of controlled songs will be subject to this agreement. Rights to license and administer controlled songs will be subject to this agreement.

F) You will give us mechanical licenses on all songs written or composed by you in the masters under this agreement. The rates and terms are to be similar to the license issued by the Harry Fox Agency, Inc. If the rates and terms are more than the Harry Fox Agency the excess will come out of your royalties.

11) GRANT OF NAME AND PICTURE

A) You give to us the right to use your name, picture, and life story for business purposes. This use will be related to the recordings made under this agreement. We may use this right throughout the world. We may give this right to others to use.

12) ACCOUNTING

A) Your royalty statements will be sent every six months. January to June will be sent by September 30th. July to December will be sent by March 30th. You will receive payment of royalties earned by you. Advances and charges under this agreement will be subtracted.

B) We have the right to keep in reserve some of your royalties to cover charges, credits, and returns. In the first accounting period the reserve will be fifty percent (50%). In the second accounting period the reserve will be thirty percent (30%). Thereafter it will be ten percent (10%).

C) Our licensees to sell records must pay us before we pay your royalties. We pay for the accounting period in which sales occur and statements and payments are received from our licensees.

D) Each payment by us to you will be made by one company check, payable to "Velvet Toothache," and mailed to your address above.

E) A Certified Public Accountant working for you at your expense may examine our books. The CPA may look at the books related to this agreement up to two (2) years after the statement in question. The CPA must give us thirty (30) days written notice and do his work during normal business hours at our place of business. We will do this just once a year and only once for each royalty statement. If you take us to court, it must be within three (3) years of the royalty statement.

13) WARRANTIES

A) You have the right to assign, convey, grant, and transfer to us all the rights set forth in this agreement. You have not sold, assigned, leased, or in any other way limited the rights granted to us in this agreement. No song or any part of it imitates, copies, or breaks the legal rights of others. Your recordings are "works for hire" under the United States Copyright Act.

B) You have not given to any third parties other rights not in accord with the rights given to us in this agreement. You will not do this in the future.

C) You have the ability to give us the rights in this agreement and any additions to it.

D) The group name does not break any laws of copyright, trademark, privacy, libel, slander, or defamation.

E) You have the mechanical right to record the songs on the masters.

F) There are no pending lawsuits over the masters.

14) INDEMNITY

A) You will protect us from all damages and costs arising out of claims by others. The claims must be over the warranties listed above. You agree to reimburse us for any payments made by us. We may withhold royalties until the claim is settled. We will not withhold royalties if you give us a surety bond from a company acceptable to us.

B) We will give you prompt notice of any claims, and you will have the right to hire a defense lawyer at your expense.

15) CURE OF BREACHES

A) You and we have thirty (30) days after written notice to remedy any breakdown of this agreement. If you give your masters to another record company, we may legally stop them at once.

16) NOTICES

A) All notices shall be by registered mail to the band at the address listed above. Your notice to us must be sent to our attorneys: Jones and Jones, 6789 Fictitious

Blvd., Record City, California 91919, attention Harley Jones, Esquire.

17) ASSIGNMENT

A) We have the right to assign this agreement to another record company, if they will assume our obligations in this agreement. Another record company may be a corporation that merges with us by buying all our stock.

18) NO VERBAL AGREEMENTS

A) This agreement is complete. No changes can be made unless confirmed by a written statement signed by you and two (2) officers of Pretend Records.

19) INDEPENDENT CONTRACTORS

A) You and we are independent contractors. This agreement is not a partnership or joint venture. You are not our agents or employees.

20) CHOICE OF LAW

A) This agreement has been entered into in the State of California. Its legal effect will be governed by the laws of the State of California.

21) VOID PROVISIONS

A) If any provision of this agreement is ruled illegal, no other provision of this agreement will be affected. The remaining provisions will remain in full force.

22) OWNERSHIP OF MERCHANDISING ARTWORK

A) All promotional artwork created by us for use with your name or the sale of your records belongs to us. It may not be used by any other person or company without written consent. All promotional artwork created by you for use with your name or the sale of your records belongs to you.

23) SIDEMAN/BACKGROUND VOCALIST

A) You may perform as sideman or background vocalist on records of other featured artists, if it does not interfere with our agreement. You may not solo or step out. You will not receive front cover credit. Back cover credit may be in a list of instrumentalists or vocalists. Pretend Records must be given credit in all instances.

24) RERECORDING OF MASTERS

A) You may not record any of the songs in the masters under this agreement for any other record company. This is binding for five (5) years after the first United States release of our records of these songs.

25) DEFINITION OF RECORD

A) The term "record" as used in this agreement means any device that records sound for listeners to hear at a later time. The device may exist now or be invented in the future. Only sound may be recorded or sound with visual images. These records include but are not limited to reel-to-reel tapes, cartridges, cassettes, and analog or digital prerecorded tapes.

26) DEFINITION OF MASTER

A) The term "master" as used in this agreement means any original recording accepted by us for making records. The master must meet our quality standards. If it has playing time less than six minutes (6'), it is considered one master. If it has playing time between six minutes and eleven minutes fifty-nine seconds (11'59"), it is considered two masters; and so on.

27) DEFINITION OF "LP", "EP", AND "SINGLE"

A) The term "LP" as used in this agreement means any record that plays thirty-five minutes (35′) or more.

B) The terms "EP" and "single" as used in this agreement mean any record that plays less than thirty-five minutes (35′).

28) FORCE MAJEURE

A) We will not be at fault if disaster prevents us from doing our part in this agreement. Disaster may be an act of God, strike, flood, or unexpected change in government. The contract will continue in full force and effect. We will suspend for no longer than six (6) months if the record industry in the United States is not affected by the same disaster.

29) EFFECTIVE DATE

A) This agreement will not become effective until signed by you and two (2) officers of Pretend Records.

30) DEFINITION OF "YOU"

A) The word "you" as used in this agreement refers to the group known as "Velvet Toothache." It refers to each member and the group as a whole. A break of any part of this agreement by any member will be deemed a break by the entire group.

31) ADVANCE

A) If you conform to all of the parts of this agreement, we will pay you these sums at the following times. The payments will be advances on royalties. We will subtract these amounts from your royalties.

i) The sum of one thousand dollars ($1,000) will be paid by company check to "Velvet Toothache." It will be paid promptly after the agreement is signed.

ii) The sum of one thousand five hundred dollars ($1,500) will be paid by company check to "Fake's Recording Studio." It will be paid promptly after the agreement is signed.

iii) If the term of this agreement is extended, the sum of five thousand dollars ($5,000) will be paid by company check to "Velvet Toothache" promptly after our decision.

PRETEND RECORDS
(The signatures of two company officers, titles, and dates signed are placed here.)

VELVET TOOTHACHE
(The signatures of each band member, dates signed, and Social Security number of each band member are placed here.)

For Further Reading

Preparation for a Career in Rock Music
Guitar Player Magazine
20085 Stevens Creek Boulevard
Cupertino, CA 95014

Bass Player Magazine
P.O. Box 57324
Boulder, CO 80322

Modern Drummer Magazine
P.O. Box 480
Mt. Morris, IL 61054

Keyboard Magazine
P.O. Box 58528
Boulder, CO 80322

Steps to Live Performance
Chevigny, Paul. *Gigs: Jazz and the Cabaret Laws in New York City*. New York: Routledge, Chapman & Hall, Inc., 1991.
Jones, Mablen, and Colon-Lugo, Ellen. *Getting It On: The Clothing of Rock'n'Roll*. New York: Abbeville Press, 1987.

Competition for a Recording Contract
Dannen, Fredric. *Hitmen, Power Brokers, and Fast Money Inside the Music Business*. New York: Times Books, Random House, Inc., 1990.
Shemel, Sidney, and Krasilovsky, M. William. *This*

Business of Music. New York: Watson-Guptill Publications, 1990.

Life-Style of Musicians
Adler, B. *Rap: Portraits and Lyrics of a Generation of Black Rockers.* New York: St. Martin, 1991.
Goldsmith, Lynn. *New Kids on the Block.* New York: Rizzoli International, 1990.

The Job Market in Rock
Lewis, Lisa A. *Gender, Politics, and MTV.* Philadelphia: Temple University Press, 1990.
Weissman, Dick. *Music Business: Career Opportunities and Self-Defense.* New York: Crown Publishers, 1990.

Index

A
Abdul, Paula, 106
accounting
    music, 12, 114
    royalty, 59, 76
acoustician, 112
ads, newspaper, 4, 14, 95
advancement, career, 34,
    99–104
advertising, 11, 16, 32, 34, 64
    artist, 113
African Americans, 29,
    106–107
agent, 11, 16–18, 25–26, 54,
    95, 109
arranging, 21–22, 50
Artist and Repertoire (A&R),
    66–67, 68, 80, 87, 110
ASCAP (American Society of
    Composers, Authors, and
    Publishers), 75
attitude
    of aspiring musician,
        119–123
    of band, 39–40
attorney, music, 63, 78, 114
audience, types of, 40–41,
    60–61, 77
audition, 25, 30–31, 34

B
band
    auditioning with, 5–8
    character of, 92–93
    evaluation of, 8–12
    management, 9, 42

music style of, 38–40, 54, 69
    as recording artist, 76
    school, 2
    search for, 4–5
    support, 37
Bangles, The, 105
bass player, 6, 11, 16, 18, 41
Beatles, 2, 50, 108
Berry, Chuck, 28, 106
Bland, Bobby "Blue", 100
BMI (Broadcast Music Inc.), 75
bookings, scheduling, 16, 96
bookkeeping, 9, 11–16, 45, 94,
    102, 114, 124–125
Boy George, 91
Brown, James, 75
bulletin board, ads on, 4, 31, 91

C
canvassing, of record
    companies, 54, 79
Capitol Records, 44, 61
Cash, Johnny, 100
C.C. Music Factory, 107
charisma, band's, 38–40,
    91–92
Checker, Chubby, 107
club operator, 30, 31, 34, 35,
    40, 66, 86, 115
compact disc, 55, 65, 76
concert, 78, 80, 96, 101
    organizer, 115
contest, songwriting, 23, 30, 53
contract
    with agent, 17–18
    with plugger, 58

with producer, 59
    recording, 43–80
control room, 45–46
cooperation, band, 3, 7, 18, 23
copyright, 22, 73–74, 78, 103
Copyright Office, 73–74, 103
cover letter, 54
cue sheet, 19–20

D
demo (demonstration record),
    58, 66, 71, 79, 87, 96, 103
    producing, 43–52
    submitting to record
        company, 52–57
discographer, 115
distribution, 23, 52, 59–62, 64
Domino, Fats, 106
drummer, 1–2, 6, 10, 26, 36,
    41, 46, 86, 95, 103
dubs, 50–52, 79
Dylan, Bob, 100–101

E
engineer, recording, 44–52, 61,
    68, 76, 79, 109–110
Enigma Records, 60
Estefan, Gloria, 91
E Street Band, 39
ethics, questionable, 69–71
evaluation
    of band, 8–12
    of contract, 62–66, 78, 103
    of rock career, 118–129
expenses, business, 13, 25

F
fliers, 13, 31, 34, 66
45 Grave, 31
Foxx, Redd, 12
fraud, 15–16, 54, 79
Freed, Alan, 28

G
gig, playing, 2, 19, 26, 52, 94
Girl's School, 106
Go-Go's, The, 105
Gold Awards, 79
Grand Master Flash, 107
guitarist, 6, 11, 17, 36, 48, 84,
    95, 103, 122
Guns 'N Roses, 73

H
Haley, Bill, 28
Hall of Fame, 99–100, 101
Hammer, M.C., 107
Harry Fox Agency, 75
health and appearance,
    considerations of, 89–92
home base, choosing, 86–88
house, sharing, 85

I
income, 9, 13–14, 15, 25, 73
instrumentalist, 4, 19, 39, 77,
    79, 84, 87, 95, 101, 104
Internal Revenue Service, 12,
    14
international department, 72
investment, in band, 15, 17, 68
Isley Brothers, 100

J
Jackson, Janet, 106
Jackson, Michael, 79, 91, 101
jamming, 2, 5
Jeff Dahl Band, 61
Jimi Hendrix Experience, 100
jobs
    market for, 95–117
    in related fields, 111–117
    second, 82–86, 94, 95
Joel, Billy, 57

Jones, Booker T., 100
Joplin, Janis, 105

K
keyboardist, 6, 8, 36, 48, 103,
    122
King, Martin Luther, 29

L
leadership, band, 9–10
leisure, musician's, 81–82
licensing, 64
    broadcast station, 60–61
    foreign, 72
    mechanical, 59, 75, 103
life-styles, musicians', 81–94
light check, 36
Little Richard, 29
Los Angeles, 5, 16, 26, 31, 52,
    78, 86
lyricist, 21

M
Madonna, 39, 79, 106
mailings, 31–32
Mamas and Papas, 105
manager, band, 5, 9, 13, 18,
    25–28, 54, 66, 103,
    108–109, 123
marketing, 72, 116
    department, 71
    foreign, 61, 77
Master of Ceremonies (M.C.),
    10–11, 39–40, 93
McCartney, Paul, 79
mechanical fees, 75
Memphis Group, 100
Miami Sound Machine, 91
Milli Vanilli, 69–70
minorities, in rock careers,
    104–108
mixing, 50–52, 69

Money, Eddie, 73
Moore, Sam, 100
Motley Crew, 60
motor home, 25–26
music
    business, learning, 9–10,
        12–16, 73
    critic, 115
    editor, 114
    historian, 114–115
    styles of, 87
        black urban (rap), 55, 107
        dance, 21
        hard rock, 55
        heavy metal, 39, 56, 86
        punk rock, 31, 41, 55, 60
        rhythm and blues, 28–29,
            100, 106
        sheet, 57–58, 103
        trends in, 57

N
Nashville, 78, 86
Nelson, Willie, 120
networking
    business, 4–5, 11, 35, 95,
        101
    social, 89
New Kids on the Block, 39, 79
New York, 26, 52, 78, 86
Nirvana, 96
Nugent, Ted, 91

O
opportunists, in business,
    57–58

P
packaging, 59, 62, 68, 79
partnership, 11–12, 14–16, 123
performance

fees, 75
live, 25–42, 66
Phil Spitalny and His All-Girl
  Orchestra, 105
plastic records, 55, 65
Platinum Awards, 60, 79
plugger, song, 58
practice
  group, 2–3, 5, 28
  individual, 3, 5–6, 19
Prater, Dave, 100
Presley, Elvis, 28, 100, 106
press kit, 11, 34, 35, 98, 99
press release, 31–32, 34
Prince, 29, 96
producer, 51, 58–59, 61–71,
  76, 80, 110
  independent, 67, 72
production department, 71
promotion, 17, 28–35, 42, 59,
  61, 62, 97, 102, 116
proprietorship, 14–16
publicity, 72, 116
publisher, 57–58, 103, 115–116

Q
questions
  for prospective band, 15–16
  for prospective record
    company, 54–56
  self-, 127–128

R
radio station, 22, 23, 62, 72, 75,
  80, 106
  announcer, 115
  public, 61–62
record company, 14–15, 16, 18,
  23, 28, 43–80, 86, 103
  major vs. independent,
    59–62
recording artist, 73, 76

record store, 55, 72, 80
referral service, 4–5
registration, 62
  copyright, 74
  publishing, 59
rehearsal, 2, 94
  factors in, 18–21
  hall, 13, 19, 88
  room, 2, 18
rejection, handling, 7–8
relationships, supporting,
  88–89
REM, 87
royalties, 18, 23, 45, 59, 68
  publishing, 21, 74
  recording artist, 76, 80
  songwriter, 80

S
sales charts, 22, 72, 107
sales department, 72
salesperson
  band, 9, 11, 30, 102, 124
  record, 116
satisfactions, of rock career,
  125–127
sets, song, 37–38
sharks, 42, 58–59, 103
showcase, band, 34
Simon, Paul, 57
Slick, Grace, 104
Sly and the Family Stone, 77
song list, 37
songwriter, 9, 21–23, 53, 68,
  73–75, 80, 87, 102–103
Spinal Tap, 86
Springsteen, Bruce, 39
stage presence, 19, 42, 92–93
stage, setting up, 35–38
statement, income, 12–14, 87
Sting, 39
sound check, 36

studio, recording, 44–52, 79
substance abuse, 90–91

T
talents, helpful, 123–125
tape, 5–6
    cassette, 55, 65
    demo, 43
    master, 51, 59, 61, 62, 67,
        68–69, 71, 79
    monaural, 48, 51
    multitrack, 46, 48, 51
    performance, 41
tax reports, 12, 14
telephone number, permanent,
    35, 53
tickets, complimentary, 32, 67
Tom Tom Club, 106–107
Top 40 songs, 23, 38, 40, 59
tour, promotion, 67, 72
travel

arrangements, 25–28
expenses, 13

U
Ullman, Tracey, 106
union, 14–15, 35, 77

V
vault, company, 71, 113
video
    music, 106
    promotional, 68, 76
vocalist, 19, 36, 39, 48, 76

W
West, Dottie, 12
women in rock careers,
    104–108

Y
Yardbirds, 100